The Art of
Theological Reflection

The Art of
Theological Reflection

PATRICIA O'CONNELL KILLEN
and JOHN DE BEER

CROSSROAD · NEW YORK

This Printing: 2014

The Crossroad Publishing Company
www.crossroadpublishing.com

Printed in the United States of America

The publisher wishes to thank Grove/Atlantic, Inc. for use
of "The Space Crone" from *Dancing at the Edge of the World,*
copyright © 1976 by Ursula K. Le Guin.

Grateful acknowledgment to Kathleen O'Connell Sievers
for the illustrations in this book.

Library of Congress Cataloging-in-Publication Data

Killen, Patricia O'Connell.
    The art of theological reflection / by Patricia O'Connell Killen
and John de Beer.
        p. cm.
    includes bibliographical references.
    ISBN 0-8245-1401-7
    1. Theology—Methodology. 2. Faith development. I. De Beer,
John. II. Title.
    BR110.KG15 1994
230'.01—dc20   94-19384
                                                                CIP

Contents

Acknowledgments

Many people have contributed to this volume. Jack Shea and Evelyn and Jim Whitehead provided encouragement, support, and the riches of their own work in theological reflection. Tricia de Beer, Rich Brewer, Mary Kaye Cisek, Cheryl Furtak, George Gerl, Bob Hughes, Elizabeth Lang, David Killen, Michael McGinniss, Flower Ross, John Shea, Mary Ann Spina, Kathleen Sullivan-Stewart, Evelyn Whitehead, Charles Winters, Felicia Wolf, and many others have been generous conversation partners as we have developed and refined our theory of theological reflection. Tim O'Connell, former director of the Institute of Pastoral Studies, Loyola University of Chicago, provided time and space for our collaboration during the summer of 1987. Christy McKerney offered invaluable editorial comment on an early draft. David Killen, C. J. Franklin, Peter Gilmour, Judy Logue, Heidi McCormick, Franca Onyibor, Jack Shea, Felicia Wolf, and Richard Woods read the revised manuscript and provided constructive criticisms and suggestions. Mary Bader, Lisa and Allan Dreyer, Corrine and Rod Guelfi-Briggs, Maggie and Tom Horlander, Donna and Neil Jerome, Bea and Jack Kingery, and Linda and Bob Parrish read the manuscript and offered invaluable criticism as part of an ongoing parish-based adult discussion group. Kathleen O'Connell Sievers designed and drew the illustrations for the book. Justus George Lawler provided patient and insightful editorial assistance. Michael Leach and Lynn Schmitt made the final editing and production easy to negotiate. The book is stronger for these people's contributions. What weaknesses remain belong to the authors.

Introduction

> She taught me this above all else: things which don't shift and grow are dead things. They are things the witchery people want. Witchery works to scare people, to make them fear growth. But it has always been necessary, and more than ever now, it is. Otherwise we won't make it. We won't survive. That's what the witchery is counting on: that we will cling to the ceremonies the way they were, and then their power will triumph, and the people will be no more.[1]

The old Navajo healer, Betonie, directs his words to the soul-sick Tayo, but they also are for us. Betonie speaks wisely about people, their spiritual journeys, and their traditions. He knows that religious traditions are powerful, for good and for ill. He knows that religious traditions grow and change subtly as each generation sings the songs and tells the stories. He knows that freezing a tradition's practices and teachings in a rigid form enervates it. He knows that ceasing to venerate a religious tradition's wisdom and practices deprives people of the power for life their tradition embodies. He knows that losing touch with one's religious tradition in ordinary experience does the same. Finally, he knows that certain times and events challenge the capacity of the people and their heritage to empower one another.

Knowing all these things about people and their religious traditions, Betonie speaks his words to heal Tayo. His purpose is to mend the frayed threads that, when strong, weave Tayo's life and his religious heritage into a single story. Betonie wants to give Tayo back the power of his heritage so that he can live.

This book is about receiving the power of our Christian heritage so that we can live. It is about weaving the threads of our lives and our religious heritage more strongly into a single story of faithfulness through the practice of theological reflection.

When we talk about theological reflection we mean this:

> Theological reflection is the discipline of exploring individual and corporate experience in conversation with the wisdom of a religious heritage. The conversation is a genuine dialogue that seeks to hear from our own beliefs, actions, and perspectives, as well as those of the tradition. It respects the integrity of both. Theological reflection therefore may confirm, challenge, clarify, and expand how we understand our own experience and how we understand the religious tradition. The outcome is new truth and meaning for living.

Theological reflection puts our experience into a genuine conversation with our religious heritage. This conversation opens the gates between our experience and our Christian heritage. It helps us access the Christian tradition as a reliable source of guidance as we search to discover the meaning of what God is doing now in our individual and corporate lives. It assists us to clarify and deepen our relationship to the Christian tradition, especially when we struggle with its sinful and oppressive aspects. This conversation also enriches and strengthens our experiences of the tradition's sustaining wisdom and power. Further, it trains us to discern the presence of God's spirit in the social events and movements of our time.

In all these ways theological reflection develops the inherently dynamic and energy-filled relationship between our lives and the Christian heritage. Our lives and the tradition are intimately linked. If we honestly look at our lives, they lead us to the tradition. If we openly enter the tradition, it leads us to our lives.

This book grew out of the conviction that today, perhaps more than at any other time, people of faith must learn to tap the wisdom of their heritage, if the Christian tradition's powerful resources for life are to succor and sustain the welfare of human beings and the planet. Unless adult Christians engage in critical and conscious theological reflection, the Christian community's faithfulness to the gospel and its authentic witness to that gospel in the world diminishes. It even becomes counterproductive of

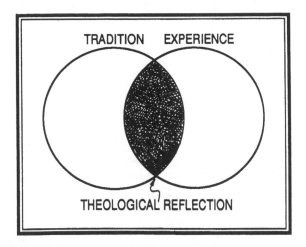

gospel values. Why? Because our capacity to comprehend and to live faithfully as Christians exists in direct proportion to our capacity to notice, describe, and discover the revelatory quality of our human experiences. Our capacity to live rich, authentic, human lives depends on our capacity to befriend and enter deeply and openly into our Christian heritage. Tapping the inherently dynamic and energy-filled connection between our lives and the Christian heritage is crucial to the survival of our world, our planet, and our church.

The intimate connection between our religious heritage and our lives makes theological reflection a vital resource for Christians who seek to experience more fully the power of their religious heritage as they seek to cooperate daily with God's actions in history. It also makes theological reflection an important resource for pastoral ministers, religious educators, spiritual directors, and all others who walk with people on their journeys in faith.

While this book is written from and about the Christian tradition because that is the authors' own, what it says about theological reflection can be extended with appropriate modifications to other religious heritages as well. Christians and members of other religious traditions seek to live faithfully in a religiously plural world. Coming to understand and appreciate one's own religious heritage is a crucial step in preparing to engage in significant interreligious dialogue with persons from other traditions.

The Human Drive for Meaning and Theological Reflection

As human beings we reflect, ask *why* about our lives, because we are drawn to seek meaning. We need meaning as much as we need food and drink. Our reflection is rooted in this human drive to understand, to make the truest and richest meaning possible of our lives.

We reflect when something happens to us that we cannot readily fit into the interpretive categories we normally use to make meaning in our lives. A question—why did you do that? A disturbance—the serious rift in a long-term friendship. An experience of beauty—hearing a poem. A transition—beginning a much desired new job. A surprising gift—finding a long-lost friend. Whatever the experience, it refuses to settle into our regular framework for interpreting life and so will not go away. It remains present in our memory and body.

All of our lives are remembered and embodied, and so are available to be explored for their fuller meaning. On the deepest level the meaning of events is never fully plumbed by us immediately. That is why the events of our lives, when nondefensively approached in reflection, can be parables for us, like the parables of Jesus.

Parables are stories that draw us in and then, through surprising shifts, unbalance us and allow us to experience and notice new perspectives on life. Parables are rich resources of insight and invitations to transformation. In theological reflection our lives become the same.

Reflection is the act of deliberately slowing down our habitual processes of interpreting our lives to take a closer look at the experience and at our frameworks for interpretation.[2] This takes courage because it makes us vulnerable in two ways: (1) we reexperience the incident—the feelings of fear, anger, awe, joy that were there. We become present in and to the event through our remembering and narrating of it. (2) We open our interpretive framework to revision so that all our most dearly held beliefs, biases, convictions, and ways of responding to life may be called into question. In this process of attending carefully to our lived experience and looking with new eyes at the categories we use to interpret life, we can be turned upside down and inside out as easily and as often as we are comforted or confirmed in how we are now living. Such is the power of parables.

Theological reflection is the process of seeking meaning that relies on the rich heritage of our Christian tradition as a primary source of wisdom and guidance. It presumes the profoundly incarnational (God present in human lives), providential (God caring for us), and revelatory (source of deepening knowledge of God and self) quality of human experience.

Because theological reflection is intimately grounded in the fundamental human drive for meaning, we anchor our presentation of it in what we have observed as the natural and almost unconscious way that people muse, reflect, and come to insight and new learnings in their lives. We call this general reflective process the *movement toward insight.* If we learn to recognize the process that has brought us to important occasions of wisdom in our ordinary lives and to see that process as the basis for theological reflection, then we will be more likely to incorporate theological reflection intentionally into our living.

Our approach to theological reflection has grown from numerous conversations about theological reflection and from experiences teaching or training theological reflection facilitators. Through the written word, John Dunne, Bernard Lonergan, John Shea, and David Tracy have contributed much to our ideas. Our presentation of theological reflection has developed most through our work as theorists and trainers for the Education for Ministry Program, School of Theology Extension Center, The University of the South, and for the former WORD program, Institute of Pastoral Studies, Loyola University of Chicago. (Education for Ministry is described in Resources for Theological Reflection.) Facilitating courses and workshops at the Institute for Pastoral Life, Kansas City, Missouri, the Center for Development of Ministry, University of St. Mary of the Lake, the Institute of Pastoral Studies, Loyola University of Chicago, and in diocesan, parish, community, and retreat settings across the United States, in the Bahamas, and in Australia and New Zealand allowed us to refine our ideas. We have used this material to teach theological reflection to thousands of people who seek to know the power of their religious heritage. That power is released when ordinary experience is brought into genuine conversation with the Christian tradition.

Chapter 1 sets the context for theological reflection by explaining the need for it and describing the standpoint from which we want to begin. Chapter 2 presents the *movement toward insight* with exercises designed to help develop awareness of it in our daily lives. Chapter 3 presents an explanation of theological reflection grounded in the movement toward insight. Chapter 4 discusses making theological reflection part of personal faith practice. It includes processes for theological reflection that an individual can use. Chapter 5 identifies the issues those who will lead theological reflection groups must consider. Chapter 6 presents guidelines for developing processes of theological reflection. Chapter 7 reviews the key elements of the theory and strategies for theological reflection that the book presents.

This book is dedicated to past and present trainers, mentors, students, and staff of the Education for Ministry Program, The University of the South, Sewanee, Tennessee; to the participants, mentors, and trainers of the former WORD program, Loyola University of Chicago; and to students, staff, and colleagues at the Institute of Pastoral Studies, Loyola University of Chicago.

1

⌒

Searching for a Way to Be Faithful

The Need for Theological Reflection

What path should I choose to live today? How can I discern a direction? How can I ground my decisions in the values that are important to me? Can I do so without coming to hate those who do not share those values, or is intolerance proof of conviction? Is there a way to find meaning in my life so that my choices do not seem random but reflect an integral pattern? Is the meaning of my life only my private possession or is it connected to others?

Sooner or later life confronts all of us with situations that raise questions like these, questions about the meaning, purpose, and value of our lives. Life experience invites us to reflect. In earlier times, before mass communication, easy travel, and extensive literacy, individuals received answers to such questions from the local community where they lived and from their religious tradition. Most often an individual's community and religious tradition were coextensive. Rarely did individuals face choices about either.

Our situation is different. We live in a global village, capable of watching victims of famine and war die on our television screens as we eat our dinner. Ease of transportation, communication technologies, extensive education, the mass media—these and more bring us regularly into contact with diverse cultures and religious traditions. The contours of our world do not allow us simply to accept answers to our questions handed down to us by communal or religious authorities. The challenges confronting us and the pluralistic world in which we live demand that we reflect on questions of meaning and value. We are called thoughtfully and carefully to make our own the answers we receive from our communities and religious traditions. This is what it means to appropriate our religious heritage critically and consciously.

Today, living on the verge of a new millennium and faced with personal, social, geopolitical and environmental choices and challenges not even imagined thirty years ago, let alone a hundred years ago, the consequences of our reflection on questions of meaning and value are momentous. The choices we make about how to live have significant impact not only for ourselves but for future generations and the planet on which we walk. Because so much is at stake, we need to pay attention to the character and quality of our reflective processes.

Traditionally, human beings asked questions of meaning and value in relationship to a religious tradition; for Christians, their Christian religious heritage. Today our pluralistic situation and the political and communal activities of certain Christian groups raise an additional question: Does the Christian tradition have anything to offer in finding the answers? Is Christianity a viable wisdom tradition as the twenty-first century dawns?

The answer is yes. It is possible to have authentic lives that reflect integral patterns grounded in values and religious wisdom. And it is possible to have such lives without using the Christian tradition as a weapon to overwhelm any and all who do not share a particular version of Christian living. This option is open to Christians who are willing to take their religious heritage seriously enough to grapple with it and their own lived experience religiously enough to entertain the possibility that God reaches out to them through it.

Authentic lives reflecting integral patterns grounded in religious wisdom and values result from seeking God's presence, not apart from the world, but in the midst of it. Seeking God's presence involves theological reflection, the artful discipline of putting our experience into conversation with the heritage of the Christian tradition. In this conversation we can be surprised and transformed by new angles of vision on our experience and acquire a deepened understanding and appreciation of our tradition. In this conversation we can find ourselves called to act in new, courageous, and compassionate ways. We are called to transformation.

Searching for meaning through theological reflection is not easy, because it does not yield the security of absolute answers. Rather, the search invites us to befriend our Christian heritage, our lived experience, our culture, and our contemporary faith community as conversation partners on the journey of faith. It asks us to hold our heritage, our culture, our community, and our own experience as companions in a conversation, a conversation where the questions and the exchange of discourse reveal new insights. Such conversation is the stuff of theological reflection. It invites us to bring our lives to the Christian heritage in a way that is liberating, challenging, and life-giving for us and for the Christian heritage.

Genuine conversation with our religious heritage is possible but not easy. Tendencies in the religious and wider culture of the United States pull us away from such interaction in two directions. The first direction, evident in growing conservative evangelical Christianity and traditionalist Catholicism, is to equate Christian faith with certitude. The second direction, evident in secular culture and some forms of liberal Christianity, is to prefer current experience to all other sources of wisdom. Neither allows for a genuine conversation with the Christian heritage. In genuine conversation participants can invest without being controlling, can wonder without needing to judge, can disagree and still appreciate the other, and can be surprised and challenged by new insights or deepened understandings and appreciations of things already known. Profound and long-lasting transformations come from this kind of reflective process.

Relating to our own experience, our culture, our faith community, and our Christian heritage in a way that allows for genuine conversation leading to wisdom connects us deeply and creatively to God's presence and purposes for us. Before looking more closely at how to do that, however, we need to consider the general standpoints from which we approach our lives and our Christian heritage. Not every standpoint—a way of acting and thinking about life—contributes equally to making genuine theological reflection possible.

The Standpoint of Certitude

Often we long for a set of rules to direct our lives clearly and effectively. A given set works for a time when we are following familiar paths and our horizons are stable. In this case we may draw on familiar precepts from our religious tradition, or from the practices and values of those around us, and rest content. But when life thrusts us into unfamiliar territory, and when our paths take us among those whose standpoints and habits are very different from our own, then our rules are often unclear or ineffective or simply contradictory.

When we find ourselves on unaccustomed ground in this way, we tend to adopt one of two very different standpoints. One is the exclusive standpoint of certitude. From this standpoint we see the unfamiliar only in terms of what we already believe. From certitude we can tolerate only that which fits our predetermined categories. If some aspect of the new landscape is too difficult to fit into the picture we wish to see, we bulldoze it until we are satisfied that the world is as we know it ought to be. This is a common human activity easy to recognize in others. Listen to a young woman describe her frustration with her father:

> I feel so sorry for the nurses at the hospital. Even though they are run off their feet, they go out of their way to pay special attention to my father and all he does is complain. During the worst of his illness I stayed with him for hours on end, and I was struck by the combination of professional competence and caring that was shown by all the staff. But to hear Dad tell it, he had fallen into the clutches of incompetent time-servers who were only interested in their paychecks. He is so certain all institutions are oppressive that he is convinced he is being wretchedly cared for, without a scrap of evidence to support this opinion.

The belief that all institutions are oppressive was formed early in her father's life. Toward the end of his life, his absolute reli-

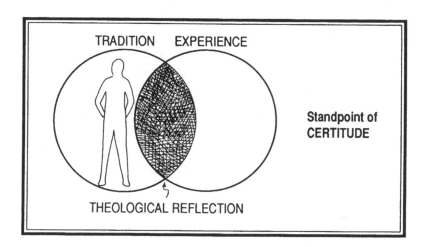

ance on this belief during a time of illness and fear prevented him from appreciating the care that was freely given.

When we operate exclusively from a standpoint of certitude, we are unable to test a new experience against the view of life that we hold. We make our current interpretation absolute, unchanging, and true. We cram everything that happens to us into that interpretation or deny experience itself. We rely on our certitude as a compass in a land thrown into turmoil by disaster, where all the guideposts are turned askew. Too often our compasses have lost their accuracy as the local magnetic fields pull them off course. Then to trust only our compass and to ignore the features of the landscape in plain sight cause us to miss the very things that we are seeking. In the example above, the certainty that all institutions are oppressive denied a sick man the comfort and solace of personal care being offered him by a particular hospital staff.

All of our certainties have this danger—that we miss the gift available to us in our experience. Religious certainties are the most costly of all. When we are certain that we understand how God is present in our world and have clearly defined the appropriate ways to respond to that presence, then our understanding becomes an idol and we fail to see God's living presence. "Your ways are not my ways," says the Lord, and when our ways are the only ways we are willing to countenance, then we miss the new things that God provides.

Our ability to miss God's presence in this way is well documented in the Hebrew Scriptures. All four Gospels of the New Testament attest to the difficulty religious people had in following the new way that Jesus was opening for them. The Acts of the Apostles contains perhaps the most extreme example of religious certitude blinding us to God's presence:

> Meanwhile Saul, still breathing threats and murder against the disciples of the Lord, went to the high priest and asked him for letters to the synagogues at Damascus, so that if he found any belonging to the Way, men or women, he might bring them bound to Jerusalem. Now as he was going along and approaching Damascus, suddenly a light from heaven flashed around him. He fell to the ground and heard a voice saying to him, "Saul, Saul, why do you persecute me?" He asked, "Who are you, Lord?" The reply came, "I am Jesus, whom you are persecuting; get up and enter the city, and you will be told what you are to do." The men who were traveling with him stood speechless, because they heard the voice but saw no one. Saul got up from the ground, and though his eyes were open he could see nothing; so they led him by the hand and brought him into Damascus. For three days he was without sight, and neither ate nor drank. (Acts of the Apostles 9:1–10)

Jolted out of his standpoint of certitude, for a while Saul was able to see nothing at all. All of his seeing had been framed by his absolute religious certitude that viewed the disciples of Jesus as blasphemers worthy of death. When the "light from heaven" flashed about him on the road to Damascus and overcame his intransigence, he was forced to ask a question, "Who are you, Lord?" Once he accepted the testimony of the voice, "I am Jesus, whom you are persecuting," Saul no longer had a way to see anything. So with us when life undermines the certitudes governing our view of the world, we no longer have a way to see. We need a whole new way of seeing.

The tendency to live from a standpoint of certitude is much more easily recognized in others than in ourselves. The 1943 Academy Award-winning film, *The Song of Bernadette*, contains a classic example. In the story, Bernadette, a simple peasant girl who has received visions of the Blessed Virgin Mary, enters a convent. She is placed under the authority of the mistress or director of novices (sisters in training) who wants desperately to be a holy woman and is certain she knows what a holy woman is. The mistress prays diligently and practices fasting, kneeling for long hours, sleeping on the floor, and other ascetical disciplines in her effort to win God's favor. She is jealous of Bernadette's vision, and the young woman's simplicity of spirit provokes the woman's rage.

In the course of her novitiate Bernadette develops a cancerous ulcer on her leg. The novice mistress dismisses Bernadette's report of the ulcer. Eventually Bernadette, who has never complained of her pain, collapses. This begins her brief period of terminal illness.

Only at Bernadette's collapse, confronted by the fact that her misguided desire for God's favor has led her to contribute to the death of another human being, does the novice mistress relinquish her certitude. She weeps bitterly when she recognizes that idolizing her own image of holiness has cost her the awareness of God's presence in her life, the knowledge of God's true will for her, and the experience of what holiness might really be.

Few among us are courageous enough to identify ourselves with the director of novices. Yet before we can set off on a journey of discovery, we must be ready to find that life will call into question our most cherished certainties. We may find our attachment to our ideas preventing the movement toward insight God wills in our lives. This is the irony of authentic faith that many Christians miss. In lusting after certitude in matters of faith so that we can be sure we are correct and on the path to God, we miss the revelatory presence of God in our often uncertain and ambiguous daily lives.

The standpoint of certitude prevails when Christians accept the Bible or official church teaching literally as God's Word, providing an absolutely clear set of directions for life. In this stance we blindly accept the rules, truths, or general principles and apply them in every situation that might arise. When we apply absolute rules to situations, we avoid having to look deeply at the situation and the people involved; to take responsibility for interpreting and acting in the situation with the eyes and heart of faith; to be responsible carriers of the Christian heritage. Acting from this standpoint we can pretend that we know certainly what God wants for every particular situation.

Approaching the Christian heritage from the standpoint of certitude creates serious problems for authentic faith. When we take this approach we never consider the degree to which we are reading our own late twentieth-century assumptions, values, and worldview into the biblical material or theological tradition. We think we are reading or hearing God's Word when, in fact, we have approached Scripture or tradition in a way that allows it only to mirror back to us the assumptions and interpretative positions we are bringing to it.

An authentic encounter with the Word of God occurs in the engagement between the text, teaching, and people in the context of a living faith community. Many contemporary First World Christians, having lost the foundational insight into how the Word of God works in a community of faith, use Scripture, lists of beliefs, or moral teachings of a particular denomination like talismans: they repeat the words or perform the rituals and insist that all will be well.

Any approach to the Christian tradition that promotes simplistic application of general biblical or religious truth statements to our lives obstructs theological reflection. To apply an already worked-out interpretation—one's own or someone else's—to a situation, without looking for the resonances between the general religious truth and our lived experience, misses God's dynamic action in present human experience.

In the standpoint of certitude we misguidedly value the Christian heritage so much that we deny God's action in contemporary experience. Often, when we work from a standpoint of religious certitude, we protect the Christian heritage fiercely. We cherish its wisdom and guidance and defend it against all who question it. We forget, however, that the focus of the tradition—God's self-revelation to human beings in history—continues. We are drawn to the certitude of God's action in the past because it seems so clear and obvious, quite unlike the uncertainty and messiness of our own lives. We long for God to do for us what God has done for our ancestors in faith, but we fear facing our own experience.

Fearing our own experience and attempting to escape into a

uniform Christian cultural consensus have equally serious consequences for our world today. Both lead to distortions of theology and misuse of the Christian tradition's wisdom. Simply applying the tradition, fitting life experience into a preestablished interpretive framework, is not theology—reflection on the experience of God—but ideology—repetition of ideas about God to support the status quo.[1] Such simplistic repetition does not create a transforming encounter with tradition. Rather it employs the tradition to reinforce current arrangements of power, values, and resources without any critical reflection on their appropriateness for the current context or their faithfulness to the message of the gospel. This ideological approach to Scripture and religious teaching diminishes our ability to mediate the richness of the Christian tradition to a world badly in need of the gospel.

Genuine theological reflection self-consciously translates tradition for our lives now and our lives for the tradition. It communicates the authority of Scripture or church teaching not as a simple external norm to be applied, but as the authority of truth disclosed to mind and heart.[2] Genuine theology is the fruit of a dynamic process of reflection.

The standpoint of certitude leads us prematurely to try to fit our experience into the tradition's interpretive framework. That framework is built from generations of Christians' experience, and we trust that it contains rich resources for our lives. But we are not ready to bring our experience to it until we have paid attention to our own experience. It is impossible to see the genuine fit between our experience and our tradition's teachings and wisdom until we have paid respectful attention to both.

In the standpoint of certitude, we deny our own experience out of obeisance to the tradition. As a result we have no ears to hear what God might be saying to us in our experience. Out of obeisance to the tradition we impoverish our own faith by which God is with us. Hence, the exclusive standpoint of certitude turns the bread and wine of the gospel into stone and vinegar. This is the cost of choosing the tradition without also choosing our experience.

The Standpoint of Self-Assurance

Sometimes our world overwhelms us with its complexity; our social, religious, and familial traditions appear unreliable, irrele-

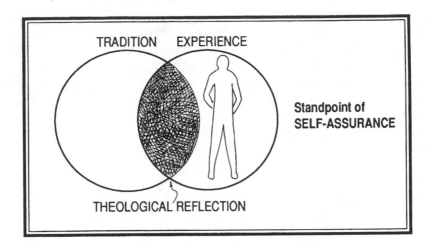

vant, or oppressive; and we fear that we cannot count on the people around us. Fed up with the frailty and fallibility of our contexts, we may decide to trust only ourselves, our own experience, how we think and feel now, in each new situation. We choose to be our own compass, map, and guide and reject our need for any other.

This may work for awhile, if our contexts remain stable. But when life presents us with new situations and we continue to rely only on our own perceptions, we can miss much. We become like Christopher Columbus who was sure that he had reached India, despite massive evidence to the contrary. This is the standpoint of self-assurance: to rely solely on my current experience and perspectives, what I think and feel now.

The late physicist Richard Feynman described an encounter with a person operating from the standpoint of self-assurance. A taxi driver in Port-of-Spain, Trinidad, raised the question of how to get out of poverty. He pointed out to Feynman that some Trinidadians who were very poor managed to send their children to college. He told Feynman that he was betting on the horses so he could get ahead. When Feynman responded that betting on horses was not the most efficient way to accumulate resources, the taxi driver insisted that it was his way, that he saw no other way, and that it could work for him.[3]

The taxi driver, trusting only his own experience, desires, and way of thinking about the world, could not hear what Feynman said. Nor would he examine the behavior of Trinidadians who were overcoming poverty for guidance in his quest. He was caught in his desire for affluence. This happens when we operate from a standpoint of self-assurance; we do not see how we are in the sway of demanding internal desires. We do not notice distortions or inaccuracies in our perspectives on life.

In the Gospels Jesus encounters people in the standpoint of self-assurance. One is the rich young man:

> As he was setting out on a journey a man ran up and knelt down before him, and asked him, "Good Teacher, what must I do to inherit eternal life?" Jesus said to him, "Why do you call me good? No one is good but God alone. You know the commandments:
> 'You shall not murder;
> You shall not commit adultery;
> You shall not steal;
> You shall not bear false witness;
> You shall not defraud;
> Honor your father and your mother.'"
> He said to him, "Teacher, I have kept all these since my youth." Jesus, looking at him, loved him and said, "You lack one thing; go, sell what you own and give the money to the poor and you will then have treasure in heaven; then, come, follow me." When he heard this, he was shocked and went away grieving for he had many possessions. (Mark 10:17–22)

In this story Jesus interacts with the rich young man to undermine his overwhelming confidence in his own power so that he might be open to the power of the kingdom of God. In his first response, "Why do you call me good?," Jesus undercuts the young man's confidence in his judgment of other people's performance. Such an orientation does not lead to attentive discernment of God's action. But the young man misses the point. He does not catch what Jesus is trying to teach him about making judgments based on his own self-assurance.

Then Jesus recites the stipulations of the law:

You shall not murder;
You shall not commit adultery;
You shall not steal;
You shall not bear false witness;
You shall not defraud;
Honor your father and your mother.

This evokes only a confident response from the young man, that he has managed since childhood to keep the commandments entirely. The young man does not realize that he is claiming to have done the impossible. So, Jesus goes one step further to try to unbalance the young man. Jesus tells him to sell what he has, give the proceeds to the poor, and come follow Jesus. Jesus' directive makes the young man sad because he has many possessions. It seems not to crack his invisible prison of self-assurance.[4]

The young man wants eternal life, but he wants it on his own terms. He is mired in his own view of how to attain it, a view that keeps him in control. He chooses to keep the commandments. These are rules he wants to follow because doing so, he believes, makes him righteous. But when it comes to embracing poverty and following Jesus, that takes the control away from him. That leaves him open and vulnerable in ways he cannot tolerate.

Jesus invited the rich young man to live the Law or Torah fully, to love his neighbor as himself by selling what he had and joining the community of those who long for God's kingdom. The rich young man chose to retain his own understanding of Torah, one that left him in control.

Keeping ourselves in control is one of the seductive qualities of the standpoint of self-assurance. When in this standpoint, we often create agendas for ourselves, whether these consist of maintaining all our options or achieving a fiercely desired goal. We are tempted to become calculating in the way we relate to people, information, and activities, always considering them in terms of how they benefit us or our goal. In the standpoint of self-assurance our projects—family, work, creative ventures— easily become idols that serve only our own desires to be righteous, to see ourselves as good and worthy.

We are tempted to overconfidence and control in the standpoint of self-assurance because this standpoint dulls our awareness of how much we are shaped by our contexts and communities. We forget or deny our need for the resources of language, culture, physical sustenance, and more that we have inherited from past generations. We ignore the limits or givenness of much of our life—economic, familial, social, religious. We do not recognize how much our thoughts and feelings in situations are informed by what we have learned from our cultures. In the standpoint of self-assurance we think of our lives as primarily our own projects and consider our social contexts and our traditions primarily as burdens to be overcome or manipulated for our benefit.

Some people in the standpoint of self-assurance reject the Christian tradition and all inherited traditions out of hand as less trustworthy than their own immediate experiences, thoughts, and desires. When Christians act in this standpoint they often judge or denigrate the tradition, or reinterpret it into something else so that it reinforces their beliefs and desires when, in fact, it does not. In the standpoint of self-assurance we look in the tradition only for support of what we now think. This approach denies the tradition's integrity and blocks our openness to the tradition's revelatory power.

In the standpoint of self-assurance we ignore the fact that the tradition offers us ways to perceive our experience and to interpret it. We miss the degree to which our religious tradition can expand our experience and correct distortions in our perception of it. We can forget that the tradition exists to put us in touch fully with reality.

Ironically, when we operate from the standpoint of self-assurance we often chide those who cling to the tradition in quest of certitude, accusing them of submitting themselves to outmoded external authorities. What we do not see is how much our own standpoint of self-assurance is a quest for certitude through self-reliance.

Cost of Certitude and Self-Assurance

The standpoint of certitude costs us our experience in order to possess the tradition. The standpoint of self-assurance costs us the richer meaning and understanding that the Christian tradition has to offer in order to make our current thoughts, feelings, and desires primary.

The problem with both certitude and self-assurance as exclusive standpoints is that they diminish our ability to relate to ourselves, our experience, our world, and our religious heritage. They lead us to deny or exaggerate our capacities as individuals and communities and to idolize or deny the reality of the traditions in which we come to awareness as human beings. From the standpoint of certitude alone we deny ourselves and our present experience in obeisance to an idealized past that we tell ourselves will save us if we simply submit. From the standpoint of self-assurance alone we deny the limits of much of our lives, our embeddedness in family, culture, and traditions and act as if we can construct our lives in their entirety.

The exclusive standpoints of certitude and self-assurance do not empower reflective, committed, compassionate lives. They lead us to repeat some of the tradition's teachings out of context in order to support particular arrangements of power, values, and roles that we hold dear and from which we benefit. They lead us to ignore other aspects of the tradition for the same purpose. Repetition and dismissal leave us deaf and blind to the resources of the Christian tradition and to the content of our current experience. Both act as a barrier between us and God's presence, power, and purpose. They block the ability of we who call ourselves Christians to mediate the compassion, love, justice, healing, forgiveness, and reconciliation of Jesus Christ for others. They seduce us into believing that life will not call into question our most cherished certainties. They obstruct growth in wisdom or understanding. Neither standpoint alone leads to a liberating encounter with God's Word in the tradition or in human experience.

Precisely because these two ways of understanding dominate discussions of individual and corporate values and spirituality in our culture and in our churches, we are in desperate need of authentic theological reflection. Without theological reflection, faith becomes something that belonged to the forebears of the tradition and currently is protected by the sanctioned theological experts. Faith is reduced to a possession. Faith serves as a justification for what we already think, religious code language to legitimate whatever psychological, sociological, economic, or political theory that we hold.

In the standpoint of certitude we protect fiercely the memory of the experience of God handed down from our religious forebears. All too frequently, however, we have not a clue what our religious forebears experienced and intended to convey to us because we are not aware of it in our own experience. In the standpoint of self-assurance we pay attention to our experience but miss many of its elements and its richer meaning because we do not trust that our forebears' wisdom adds anything to our experience.

Without authentic theological reflection we Christians cannot achieve the personal maturity and integrity appropriate to us. Theological reflection that involves heart and mind, consciousness and activity, provides a discipline in the life of faith. It enables us to integrate seemingly irreconcilable realms of activity and knowledge in our lives. As adult Christians we are called to more than mindless obedience to authority or totally self-determined thought and action.

Without authentic theological reflection we cannot exercise fully the ministry appropriate to us as baptized Christians. As the values of First World cultures increasingly undercut both humanistic and Christian visions it is crucial that we claim and present our faith in a manner that has integrity and is intelligible. Our presentation must be faithful to the fullest reading of the tradition, including the experience of the present community of faith. This gives it integrity. It also must make sense to any who, for the sake of discussion, will grant the presuppositions of faith. This makes it intelligible. The alternatives to presenting the faith in an intelligible fashion and with integrity are a certitude that turns gospel bread into stone or a self-assurance that reduces the individual to an isolated, self-contained, diminished being.

The complexity of our present situation makes it urgent that adult Christians learn to think, to feel, and to perceive faithfully. We must be able to engage the tradition in conversation so that we can bring its wisdom to bear powerfully in our lives and our worlds.

If authentic theological reflection cannot happen, if the Christian tradition's only value is to bolster and baptize social, economic, and political conventions, then it is dead or, worse, demonic. To ignore or actively to oppose the tradition when it is used in this way may seem to be the only options. But they can be costly ones. Ignoring or opposing the tradition can lead us to miss the wellspring of life in the Christian heritage. There is a continuing creative and faithful vitality within the Christian heritage that can renew the tradition and fund the lives of communities and individuals. This vitality can be tapped when people engage the tradition in genuine conversation, when they practice theological reflection.

The Standpoint of Exploration

The alternative to the exclusive standpoints of certitude and self-assurance is a standpoint of exploration. Sometimes we break out, or are jolted out, of our habitual tendency to see only what fits our preconceived notions or to rely only on our immediate responses. At this point we may move into the standpoint of exploration if, instead of landscaping the ground to our own taste, we attempt to discover where we are and how we are to proceed. What sources are we to consult? How can we locate and draw appropriately on the wisdom contained in the Christian Scriptures and teachings? How can we test the value of our previously held positions in the new situations in which we find ourselves? How can we make use of modern scientific frameworks without abandoning our commitment to understand our place in life primarily as followers of Jesus? When we understand ourselves as explorers charged with finding our way as disciples of Jesus in our time and place, how shall we proceed?

When we are confused we tend to wander blindly, not actually seeing where we are going. We may cross the same ground several times before the realization creeps into our awareness, "I seem to have been here before. Could I really be going in circles?" This inability to notice the details of our surroundings is true whether we have become disoriented in a forest, in a city, or in a relationship. Thus, the first step in finding our way is to pay careful attention to where we are. If we pause to describe the territory in as much detail as possible, the territory itself will

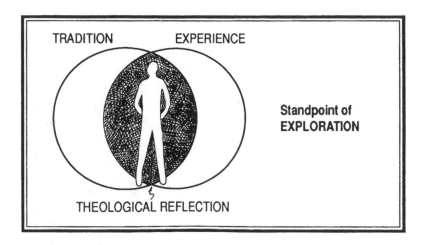

often present us with a clue for further exploration. This is especially true when we are confused by what we are experiencing, and puzzled as to how best to respond to situations that confront us. When we enter into our experience and describe from inside the evidence of our senses, we may find ourselves caught up in a movement of discovery, what we are calling the *movement toward insight.* Following this movement will lead us on new paths and change our ways of understanding the world and our place in it.

Living from a standpoint of exploration in this way draws us into community. In a paradoxical fashion, as we increasingly enter our own experience as a first step in the movement toward insight, both our desire and our need increase for companions and for sources of wisdom from outside ourselves that can help us interpret our experience.

This need is an essential part of the story of Saul on the Damascus road. Saul depended on the men who were traveling with him to bring him into the city. In his blindness, he was unable to continue alone. Once in the city, he did nothing, not even eat or drink, until Ananias laid hands on him and said,

> "Brother Saul, the Lord Jesus, who appeared to you on your way here, has sent me so that you may regain your sight and be filled with the Holy Spirit." (Acts 9:17)

Ananias affirmed the experience Saul had on the road, offered him an understanding consistent with that experience, and provided confidence that the time was now ripe for Saul to see life in a new way, filled with the Holy Spirit.

In the earlier example of the young woman's hospitalized father, the man was not able to enter a standpoint of exploration. This left him isolated and unable to receive the rich gifts of the caregivers who tended him. He could not see life in a new way. Neither could the Trinidadian taxi driver nor the rich young man in Mark's Gospel imagine alternatives to their ways of perceiving and conceiving their situations.

As explorers, we enter our experience not knowing the hidden thoughts we will discover, the feelings that will arise, the images we will encounter, the questions we will endure, or the insights that will guide us. This is theological reflection—to allow the thoughts, feelings, images, and insights that arise from the concrete events of our lives to be in genuine conversation with the wisdom of the entire Christian community throughout the ages.

Theological reflection opens for each contemporary Christian the reality of the claim that God's presence, power, and purpose work for us in our time as they operated for our ancestors in faith in their time. The conversation between our life experiences and the Christian tradition can be honest and genuine because we trust this truth. But that conversation can only take place when we allow the questions to assume primacy and set aside our fears. In such conversation we are carried into understanding, which is a gift that comes to us, not a prize that we achieve.

Summary

Sooner or later life confronts us with situations that raise questions about the meaning, purpose, and value of our lives. How we answer those questions has significant consequences for us personally, for our world, and for our planet. As Christians we want to answer questions about the meaning, purpose, and value of our actions faithfully. In our complex world being faithful requires being open to God's presence in our experience and in our Christian heritage.

We need the healing the gospel offers. Our complex and broken world desperately needs it too. It takes Christian adults who are mature in their faith and in touch with the power of their heritage to bring that healing word and presence to family, marketplace, community, nation, and planet.

Theological reflection nurtures growth in mature faith by bringing life experience into conversation with the wisdom of the Christian heritage. To practice theological reflection we must be able to pay attention to and inquire about the meaning of our individual experiences, our world, and our religious heritage. The standpoints of certitude and self-assurance block our ability to do so. The standpoint of exploration supports it. Transformative theological reflection takes place in the standpoint of exploration.

2

∾

The Movement Toward Insight:
The Human Process
of Coming to Wisdom

For human beings the drive for meaning, the drive to have
what we encounter, endure, create, feel, and think in our lives
make sense in an integrated manner, rivals the drive for physical
survival. When we reflect on, muse over, ponder, or analyze
events we are engaged in the process of making meaning.

The process of making meaning has a structure to it, though
most of us move through the process without noticing its structure. This is because our drive is to find meaning in our lives.
Asking how we do so is a different kind of activity.

Our work with theological reflection groups led us to ask how
human beings make meaning when they reflect. In training sessions and theological reflection groups we observed a pattern to
the process by which people came to significant insights. Key
elements of this pattern were present in the process of reflection
regardless of the particular method of theological reflection we
used. We call this pattern in the process of reflection the *movement toward insight.*

The movement flows through five parts: experience, feelings,
images, insight, and action. Think of them as related in a circular
spiral: action, by leading to new experiences in our lives, propels
us back to experience. The movement is this:

When we enter our **experience,** we encounter our **feelings.**

When we pay attention to those **feelings, images** arise.

Considering and questioning those **images** may spark **insight.**

Insight leads, if we are willing and ready, to **action.**

Becoming aware of this movement in our own lives can strengthen and refine our habit of reflection. It puts us in touch with how, at times in our lives, we have come to significant understandings that allowed us to choose more freely among options or that strengthened or shifted our sense of who we are in relation to God, self, other, and the world.

Experience

Defining Experience

Experience is what happens to us; what occurs in which we are active or passive participants. Experience has an inner dimension—the feelings, thoughts, attitudes, and hopes that we carry into and out of any situation. This inner dimension involves our response to and what we make of and do with what occurs. It accents how we experience events and situations. Experience also has an outer dimension involving the people, places, projects, and objects that surround us and with which we interact. The outer dimension accents what we experience.

Experience, with its inner and outer dimensions, is a constant, dynamic flow. We can think of experience as the flow between our selves and the various places, issues, situations, ideas, and problems with which we interact.[1]

Most of our life experience goes by unnoticed. Sooner or later, however, something happens that causes us to become more aware of our experience. A vista of incredible beauty, the sound of exquisitely delicate music, the embrace of a small child, intense physical pain, these experiences and countless others like them invite us to reflect. They enter our lives in small ways, like receiving an unexpected thank-you note, or in massive ways, like com-

ENTER INTO THE EXPERIENCE

ing home and finding our house burning. These experiences disrupt the taken-for-granted measure of our existence. They lead us to confront the question of meaning in our lives.

Entering Experience

We begin to reflect by reentering our experience. So the first step for reflection is to be aware of what we are in fact experiencing. This awareness includes attention to the inner and outer dimensions of our experience and a careful attempt to describe both accurately.

Two people walking together can have quite different experiences of the same city street; pedestrians who attract one person may alarm the other, stores that draw one person's lingering attention may not receive a second glance from the other. Our experience is influenced both by our external environment—the outer dimension—and by what we bring to it, the inner environment—our aspirations, fears, expectations, and predispositions. The same rainstorm may be experienced by a farmer as providential, by a commuter as hazardous, and by the host and hostess of a garden party as disastrous. These differing interpretations result from varied combinations of inner and outer environments for the persons involved.

Sometimes we are particularly aware of what is happening around us and within us. When we know that we are seeing a familiar place for the final time, for example, we may notice the details of architecture, the quality of the light, the background noise, and at the same time notice the thoughts and feelings that rise up in us as we look and listen. We are keenly aware of both the inner and the outer dimensions of our experience. In these situations we are also, in a paradoxical way, aware of self, of the self that has been a part of this place and now is moving on. At such moments we live right inside our experience. This is the position from which we best reflect—from right inside our experience.

For most of us, this heightened awareness is the exception rather than the rule in our lives. Often the events we ponder are those during which we were so preoccupied with our own expectations and judgments that we were not aware of either the internal or the external dimensions of our actual experience. We have an intuitive sense that we do not comprehend the event. We know that our interpretive frameworks have been inadequate, but we do not know how. Often we cannot disengage our interpretive process sufficiently to retrieve the original event.

In this situation we find ourselves turning the event over seemingly endlessly in our minds. In our mulling, if we stop to notice, we discover that what repeats endlessly in our minds is a cluster of judgments and interpretations, coded for us by words such as "should," "ought," "never," "always," "if only." These block our access to experience. When we remember or retell an event this way it is cluttered with already formed interpretations—interpretations that do not fit. If they did, the event would not be remaining with us, nagging for further attention.

To reenter our experience, then, we need to pay attention to how we tend to edit severely or rewrite its content for circulation to others and to ourselves. For example:

> A couple prepared together for months for the birth of their first child. They shared the actual delivery of the child as intimately as possible. The husband stood close by, timing the

contractions, coaching his wife's breathing, doing whatever he could to participate actively in what was happening. When the miracle of birth occurred, and the infant was laid in her mother's arms, he wanted to share in her experience of absolute relief and delight. In fact, he felt rather flat. Only months later could he admit to himself that as he saw his daughter in his wife's arms he experienced himself as displaced, abandoned, and felt a strong surge of jealousy.

It took the man some time to acknowledge the full range of his feelings and thoughts in the situation because they did not match what he had expected and wanted them to be. His preestablished interpretive categories interfered with his ability to attend to and to be aware of his experience.

For reflection that leads to insight, we need to reenter our experience openly, so that it is fresh, slightly unfamiliar, and thus a potential source of revelation. We want to reenter openly all events on which we reflect, even well-worn ones. Revelation brings newness, even to incidents and truths we have long known. The key to entering experience in this way is to narrate it, to describe it, not cram it into a preconceived interpretive framework.

Story or narrative has a dramatic quality that enables narrator and listeners to enter into the experience being described. Through the particular description of both the internal and external dimensions of a specific experience we are drawn into it and become aware of its energized aspects. From this center we can reflect on our own lives and on the lives of those who share their experiences with us.

A narrative description of a concrete human experience intensifies that experience in a way that makes it begin to resonate with and relate to the stories of others. This resonance does not occur on the level of the particular topic of the story. It sounds on a deeper, symbolic level where the quality of the particular event, conveyed in the dominant feelings that were experienced in it, relate us to the humanness of all events characterized by such feelings. A narrative description of an event, then, can reveal the profoundly symbolic and interrelated quality of our lives. We want to learn how to perceive this.

In the first step of the movement toward insight, we enter our experience by narrating or describing it. We remember it as accurately as we can, both the inner subjective and the outer elements, by constructing a narrative or a story that captures both as accurately as possible. The classic guidelines of telling "who" did "what," "when," "where," and "how," provide the outline.

Simple concrete description connects us to our five senses. The data of our senses enriches the description. Sufficiently textured description of the inner and outer elements of the event makes the narrator present to the experience again. It also allows companions in a reflective process imaginatively to enter our experience as well. The rule for telling an incident for reflection is to tell enough for ourselves and others to see what we saw, feel what we felt, smell what we smelled, experience the fear, joy, peace that we knew. Concrete, real, accurate description honors human experience and disposes us to be able to hear what God might be saying to us through it.

The question to be suspended at this stage of the movement toward insight is the question *why*. Answering *why* yields an interpretation of an event. Whatever our interpretation is at the beginning, it is most likely inadequate and unsatisfying, or we would not be reflecting on the situation. Answering *why* too soon smothers the actual experience. It prematurely distances us from the event and rationalizes what happened. This short-circuits the revelatory power of the experience. God cannot speak to us if we refuse to be present—nonjudgmentally aware and attentive— to our experience. We cannot be nonjudgmentally present to our experience if we are focused on our interpretation of it, instead of on the event.

Premature interpretation of experience is something we encounter in many settings. Recall your experiences in a faith-sharing or other small-group discussion. Have you ever found yourself feeling bored, angry, or irritated when listening to others speak? Odds are, if you did, that you were hearing the telling about experience from a prematurely distanced and rationalized stance. An entire value system and interpretive framework were laid over the event. The meaning was already controlled by the telling, and you could only agree or disagree with the interpretation; nothing was left to discover. That way of telling does not invite others in, does not ask our exploration; it is certain, and set, and boring. It repeats a fully worked out interpretation but one which does not fit the event. It acts as a barrier between the teller, listeners, and the actual event with its revelatory potential.

Reentering our experience requires practicing the discipline of narrating what has happened to us as fully as possible. We set the scene, inner and outer, with clear description. We honor ourselves and our companions in reflection by accepting non-judgmentally the reality of our experience and narrating the event in that accepting, nonjudgmental way. We withhold the judgments, withhold self-berating or self-congratulatory beliefs, and simply attend to the event. The goal here for the narrator is not some perfect objectivity, for that cuts us off from the experience; rather, the goal is attentive subjectivity, being present to our experience, recalling and narrating it as accurately and honestly and nonjudgmentally as possible. The goal for listeners, if we reflect with companions, is the same nonjudgmental, attentive subjectivity.

Practicing Nonjudgmental Narration

Learning to narrate our experience in a richly descriptive and nonjudgmental manner is an important discipline in the spiritual life and one that takes practice. Remember that in reflection we want to slow down our interpretive processes. We want to describe the event and not, for the moment, what we think it means or our judgments about it. The following exercises can help in beginning to practice this fundamental skill for reflection:

1. Recall an event from the past week that has minimal emotional energy for you. Write down the event in the order in which it happened, avoiding any judgments, for example, sentences that use the words "should," "ought," "if only" and others like them. Review the narration and eliminate judgments about the intentions, motivations, or purposes

of other people in the event. Do you have a simple, non-judgmental description?

2. Recall an event from the past month in your life about which you have strong feelings. Write down this event in the order in which it happened, paying attention to its inner and outer dimensions. Include a description of your feelings in the narration. You may also include the thoughts that were running through your mind, but label them as such. Write only what happened. Avoid judgments. Do not justify, explain, or analyze the event; these are interpretive activities, and you want to put interpretation on hold as much as possible for the time being.

3. Read your narration out loud to yourself. Notice how your body feels and what your emotions are as you do so.

4. Identify what is difficult, challenging, rewarding, exciting about simply narrating your experience.

Feelings

Defining Feeling

When we enter our experience—narrate it nonjudgmentally and attentively—we find it saturated with feeling. This is because our capacity to feel, to respond with our entire being to reality, is the essence of our nature as enfleshed spirits. Our feelings exemplify the human drive for meaning, a drive that the Christian tradition understands as the desire to know reality intimately, and ultimately to know God.

Feelings are our embodied affective and intelligent responses to reality as we encounter it. We are both intelligent and bodily and so are our spontaneous responses to reality. Feeling joins body and mind. This means that feeling responses are the most human responses to reality.[2]

Feelings, then, are an important component of the movement toward insight. They are clues to the meaning of our experience. We cannot have transformative insights without them. In the movement toward insight we consider them to be gifts. They

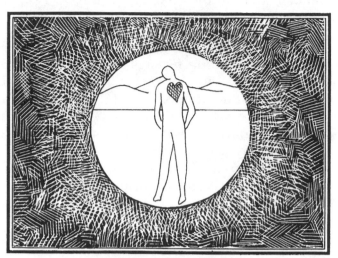

ENCOUNTER FEELINGS

incarnate questions, values, and wisdom that we are living, but which we cannot yet articulate and of which we may be unaware.

Feelings are rich resources in our journey to meaning. When we encounter a particular feeling in our experience, we want to think of it as neither inevitable, nor fleeting, nor eternal; we do not want to cling to it or control it, but simply to experience the feeling, to notice it, and reflect on it.

True feelings are intimately connected to the sensations of our bodies. Unless we can locate an identified feeling in our body, and our whole body is involved, we have not named a feeling. For example, if I feel anxious, I can describe the tenseness in my muscles, the queasiness in my stomach, or other sensations that commonly accompany anxiety. Or, if I am happy, I can describe the relaxed and energized sensation of my body.

Sometimes, though, we confuse interpretive judgments about ourselves with statements of feeling. This blocks the movement toward insight because it cuts us off from our true feelings, from attending to what our experience actually is. For example:

> Anna arrived at her theological reflection group visibly distraught. When a member of the group asked her how she

was she answered, "All right." The member persisted, "How does your body feel right now?" Anna stopped, breathed deeply, and responded with tears welling up in her eyes, "I feel tense and apprehensive." She went on to report a phone conversation with her mother's physician in which he told her that her mother's cancer was active again after a two-year remission.

Anna's statement, "all right," did not express her true feelings. It was an inadequate interpretation of her experience that day, one which her body and tone of voice easily betrayed.

A true feeling always includes a physical sensation. When we locate feeling in our bodies, when we locate the physical sensation that is its source, then a feeling is named. We need a rich and specific language of feeling to relate to ourselves and to our humanity. Richness and specificity in the naming of feeling is essential to the movement toward insight. It grows naturally from the descriptive narration of our experience.

While grounded in bodily sensation, a true feeling is more than that. Besides sensation or bodily agitation, feeling involves our affective response to what is felt, our relationship to it. For example, watching a gifted athlete perform can be thrilling, but our response is more than the physical sensations of being thrilled. It involves delight and appreciation of excellence too, whether or not we express that in conceptual language. Or standing in line behind a harried young mother who handles her young child roughly may evoke anger and sadness in us. Our response entails more than the bodily sensations of anger and sadness. It involves at least implicit knowledge that such treatment harms children, sympathy for the mother's plight, and may impel intervention to distract the mother or in another way defuse the situation.

Feelings in Reflection

A feeling response to a situation is potent with meaning, even when we are not able immediately to state it. In reflection we intend to let that potential meaning emerge. But our human drive for meaning is so strong that it can disrupt reflection. Our habitual interpretive processes can lead us to misinterpret our experience by too quickly putting a meaning on it. When we do not allow ourselves to encounter our feelings, do not let them be part of our reflective process, we miss the true meaning of our experiences. True meaning emerges from reflection. It is never the result of taking the meaning of one experience and putting it onto another one.

When we bring a particularly powerful or disturbing event to reflection, we may have difficulty identifying our feelings in the experience. Indeed, when reflecting on such an incident we may have difficulty even getting the sequence of actions in order. The amount of energy, potentially revelation, that our story contains may block our ability to order events and name feelings. When this happens we need the support of companions in the reflective process. Companions can listen to the incident and ask enough clarifying questions to establish the scene clearly and describe the action in the sequence that it occurred. Then the companions can help us to identify feelings by suggesting the ones that they noticed in our story and by helping us to connect feeling and body sensation.

For reflection that leads to insight, then, narrating experiences leads to rich description of feeling that is tied to body sensation. This is essential because the feelings carry the questions, values, and wisdom embedded in our narratives and that we may not know how to articulate. Feelings carry the questions that we are living and they carry the key to their answers.

The task at this point in the movement toward insight where we encounter our feelings is to pay attention to them in an accepting manner, to befriend and welcome them, however pleasurable or uncomfortable, as the message bearers. In such reflection we notice feelings not as problems and not as something to be avoided or fixed or judged. We experience them as carriers of, incarnations of, the questions, values, and wisdom that we do not yet know how to speak. Feelings are the gift of embodied but unarticulated wisdom.

Naming Feelings: A Spiritual Discipline

An essential practice of Christian asceticism for our time is learning to name our feelings precisely, accurately, and nonjudgmentally. Feelings are of the essence of our nature as embodied spirits. We cannot deny or ignore them in the life of faith. This discipline of faith, however, is a countercultural act.

Our First World culture views feeling primarily as a problem. We are tempted to avoid feeling by denying our feelings; eating, drinking, or spending excessively; projecting our feelings onto other people or situations; or hiding from them behind free-floating anxiety or guilt.

We fear our feelings primarily because we cannot control them and we live in a culture where control is highly valued. The uncontrollability of feelings makes them scary and prob-lematical. The experience of an intense feeling, be it pain, hostil-ity, or joy, involves losing control, being vulnerable, noticing forces that transcend but impinge upon us. Experiencing our feelings requires us to give up the pretense of being able to predict the outcome of events. Feelings are the evidence denying the illusion that we are able to control events, people, and our-selves totally through reason, prediction, and planning.

When the cultural imperative to be in control grabs hold of our interpretive processes, we are susceptible to two feelings, anger and depression. When we overcommit or become exces-sively stressed, we know them both. True anger and depression are responses to rupture in our relationships—with ourselves, our communities, and our world. Too seldom, however, do we let their particular meaning for us emerge in reflection. Instead, our overactive interpretive processes prevail and lead us to mis-taken understanding of these feelings. Misinterpreted, anger and depression give the illusion of individuality and integrity. The deadening numbness of depression insulates us from the vulnerability of experiencing the full range of human feelings. When anger bursts through, it focuses and funds the fight for self-interest. Both are efforts at maintaining control. When the feelings of anger and depression are inaccurately interpreted, they cut us off from the meaning of our experience.

If the valuing of control leads us toward anger and depression, it more aggressively leads us away from joy. Joy is an exquisitely delicate feeling. It softens us and opens us to ourselves and our world. These qualities make joy a fearsome feeling. When joy pulses through our bodies we know the fragility and wonder of creation and are keenly aware of how those two qualities cannot be split apart.

Even the expression of feelings in a First World culture can be a means for avoiding feeling them. Which of us has not encountered someone who emoted at us ad nauseam, yet we came away with the sense that we never really knew what they were feeling? They spewed forth statements about being angry or anxious or upset or peaceful, but we never got the clean and simple naming of a feeling. We can use the language of feeling to insulate ourselves against feeling. We want to guard against this in our reflection.

When we consider feelings as problems, we seek to avoid them. If there are some we like to experience, we try to maintain them, to cling to them, as if they were a possession. Feelings we want to avoid we call bad, those we want to possess we call good. It is not humanly possible, though, to avoid feelings or to experience them on demand. When we conceive of feelings as things that can be avoided or possessed we distance ourselves from true feeling. This diminishes our person and stunts our capacity to be human because it blocks our ability to reflect.

Practicing Noticing and Naming Feelings

We can enhance our awareness of God's revelatory presence in our life and our skill for reflection by paying heed to our physical sensations and feelings during the day. Here are some ways to do so:

1. When you wake up in the morning, before your first coffee break, right after lunch, at your midafternoon break, and in the evening before you go to bed, take a minute to breathe deeply, quiet yourself, and notice the physical sensations of your body. What words describe your physical sensations from the tip of your toes through the center of your trunk, to your eyes and scalp? Name to yourself your sensations and how you feel. Notice what happens when you do so.

2. When you find yourself in a situation in which you are angry or agitated, take a deep breath and notice your phys-

ical sensations. Ask yourself, what are these sensations really? You may find that "angry" and "agitated" are covering more nuanced feelings, like apprehension, concern, disappointment, betrayal, which your body can reveal to you. Letting your body help you to name your feeling accurately helps you to keep from being stuck in your feelings and can give you insight into your situation.

3. The next time you catch yourself responding to a question about your feelings with a judgment, stop and ask yourself: what are my body sensations right now?

Paying Attention to Those Feelings: Journeying from Feeling to Image

Our feelings in any experience carry energy. They embody a holistic response to our existence and are a source for creativity. The feelings that accompany our experience are the carriers of unspoken, unrecognized questions, values, and wisdom and the key to their conceptualization. If we attend to those feelings as gift, they help us begin to articulate our question by leading us to an image. The image symbolizes our question by framing it one step beyond body sensation. When we allow our feeling to embody our question and then shift it to the level of image, we can begin to learn from it.

Reentering our experience fully and encountering our feelings is an undertaking both dangerous and full of promise. John Dunne captures the reason why:

> Entering into human suffering and death, I realize now, is a dangerous undertaking, especially living day after day with suffering and death weighing on your mind. It can numb you, leaving you in the cold of seeing without feeling, and it can blind you, leaving you in the dark of feeling without seeing.[3]

The problem of "seeing without feeling" characterizes mainline culture in the First World, which values objectivity and control, and so tends to deal with feeling mainly through avoidance or denial. The movement toward insight, however, leads us through the embodied life God gives us, through the feelings that arise as we stop defending ourselves against our experience by stiffening our bodies as well as our minds. No one becomes wise without learning to feel.

Even when we are willing to experience our feelings they can divert us from our reflective journey. Feelings can mesmerize and be mistaken for the final object of our reflection. For example, we can so fall in love with the feeling of love that it distorts our perception of ourselves and others. Those who become stuck in their strong negative feelings are a danger to themselves and those around them. We rightly fear someone in a *blind rage,* for example, "stuck in the dark of feeling without seeing." Similarly, someone caught in romantic self-deception is stuck in the desire for a particular feeling.

The danger, then, comes in two ways. We can be overwhelmed and mired in feelings or be deadened to them. Either makes it impossible to move toward insight and wisdom. In neither stance is it possible to hear God's Word coming through our life.

In neither stance, as well, can we tap into the energy that funds our unique contribution to life. Feelings capture the inner dimension of experience, our own internal response to what happens to us. This inner response is important, part of our own unique contribution to the human community to which we belong. Our feelings contain the energy that we are given to respond to life. But if this inward response remains altogether unformed and silent, that is, if our feelings are hidden even from ourselves, then we are unable to direct the energy they contain. Alternatively, if feelings dominate us with no understanding, they run amok and impede our ability to contribute creatively to existence.

We can bring our inner response, our unique questions, wise answers, and creative energy to the light of day when we discover the meaning in our feelings, bringing them to understanding. Then we can respond to what is happening outside us in a way that is informed and energized by the inward dimension of our experience and that is congruent with our vision of our best selves.

Practicing Attending to Feeling

Attending to our feelings means to feel them and to be aware of feeling them at the same time, without denying them or becoming mired in them. The following exercises can develop that attentiveness.

1. Recall a time in your own life when you were stuck in a feeling like anger or fear. What was it like not to be able to get out of it? How did you notice that you were no longer possessed by this feeling? Can you identify what made the shift possible?

2. Have you ever feared feeling what you felt? Did you deny the feeling? What happened when you tried to distance yourself from feelings?

3. Recall a time when you had an intense positive feeling. What happened and how did you respond when that feeling passed?

4. During ten minutes of your day, practice being aware of your feelings as you go about your regular routine.

Images

Defining Images

We give shape and voice to our feelings in the language of imagery. In normal conversation we use this process unconsciously. Our religious and literary traditions are funded by it.

Ever since my promotion I have been trying to give some shape to my new responsibilities. People come at me with so many questions that I am confused and bewildered all the time. I can't seem to see the *forest for the trees*.

This last week has been exciting and so intense that I haven't had time to think. It has been an absolute *rollercoaster ride*. A few times I thought I would be flung off.

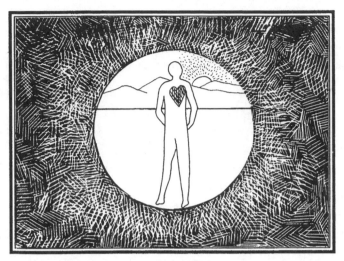

IMAGE ARISES

"How very good and pleasant it is when kindred live together in unity. It is like *the precious oil on the head, running down upon the beard . . .*" (Psalm 133:1–2)

When I read about the threat of terrorist activity I feel over-whelmed, disoriented. Its like being *trapped in a room with a fire alarm blaring.* All I can think of is to shut it off or get out.

Each of these examples describes a state of feeling in imagery that throws light on the experience. The descriptions range from idiomatic expression (forest for the trees) to fresh imagery (disoriented by a fire alarm). In either case the image retains the energy of the person's inner response while taking the next step in the movement toward insight. *Forest for the trees* retains the quality of bewilderment while suggesting a need to draw back for a while to gain perspective. *Fire alarm* suggests that real danger may be present and that shutting off the noise may not deal with the underlying problem.

The images in the examples illustrate another important point about the power of imaging in the movement toward insight. Images can be visual, tactile, olfactory, aural, savory, or some combination of these. The examples given above include all the senses. Some people consider themselves unable to form images. Usually this means that they think of imagery as only visual. All of our senses carry the power to symbolize.

The Workings of Image

Images symbolize our experience. They capture the totality of our felt response to reality in a given situation. That felt response is potent with meaning, but we often are unaware of it. Indeed, the sensations that accompany our felt response in a situation embody that unacknowledged meaning. By symbolizing our experience beyond the level of physical sensation in our bodies, our images move us toward discovering their meaning. They direct our awareness toward the experience in novel ways.

Images work like language here. We know what a word means when we can place that word in relation to other words that are similar yet have their own distinctive meaning. The meaning of a particular word is a "context" comprised of the relations of synonyms and definitions we can give for it.[4] When we symbolize our experience in an image, the image helps us begin to notice the elements of its context of meaning. An image helps us to locate our experience in relation to what we already know and to clarify what we do not know about it. An image creates a way for our experience to be included in our world of meaning, and for our world of meaning to be expanded by the new experience.

Images work differently from conceptual language, however, in being less definite and precise. Images are more total, more closely tied to our feelings, and less rationalized. Images are intelligent but not intellectualized. These qualities of images are essential to discovering the meaning of our experience in reflection. Because images are not definitive they encourage multiple aspects of meaning in an experience to come forth. They invite our gentle but active participation in the process of discovering the meaning of our experience.

An example will clarify the working of images in the process of reflection:

> Elaine worked one night each week as a volunteer in a shelter for the homeless. She found herself tense and tired at the

end of these sessions. As she reflected on her experience she described the tension she was feeling "like a steel rod across my shoulders." The image becomes a shorthand for what life was like in that situation. The image helps to explore what was going on. Steel bars are strong, capable of bearing a great load. They are also rigid rather than flexible. They are incredibly heavy, too. As Elaine named her experience in this way, she began to develop insight into the meaning of her experience and to be able to make some choices about what she would do next.

Elaine's "steel rod across my shoulders" or any other image that captures the central feeling of an experience, pleases and perturbs us, satisfies and startles us. Precisely because it does both, we are able to relate to the life experience that it symbolizes honestly, perhaps even playfully. Hence an image that captures the central feeling of an experience creates a context where we are free to gain new perspectives on that experience.

The image provides a felt connection with our experience and directs our reflective attention to it in new ways. It bears the life-energy present in the feelings of the experience and so continues our affective engagement with the original event. The image also directs our attention to the meaning of the experience by separating us slightly from the immediate intensity of the feelings the experience contained. By providing this slightly altered relationship to our experience, an image allows a different angle of vision on the situation to emerge. This combination—affective connection and an altered angle of vision—creates a climate for insight. This climate allows unnoticed meanings to rise to consciousness, new options to appear, new attitudes toward a situation to be considered.

Images invite us to relate to them. Relate is the key word here. An image that captures experience acts like a metaphor. It discloses and surprises by revealing familiar and unexpected aspects of meaning in our experience. Both broaden and enrich our awareness and understanding.

Images resist our effort to control them, suppress them, or predict their full meaning. We are inclined to do any one of the three when our overactive interpretive processes interrupt our reflection. The cost is to miss God's Word in the new experience and perhaps even to misinterpret past experiences as well. It is the culmination of following the paths of certitude and self-reliance.

Our habitual interpretive processes also can block reflection in another way, by leading us inappropriately into problem-solving and psychological analysis. Valuable in their own contexts, both problem-solving and psychological analysis are misguided when employed as primary avenues to meaning. For example, return to Elaine at the shelter for the homeless. Elaine might have begun problem-solving by brainstorming ways to eliminate the unpleasant stress in her volunteer situation. She might have found strategies to relieve her tension, but this approach would not give her the meaning of her experience. Or Elaine might have engaged in psychological analysis, by exploring what incidents from her past led her to take on difficult volunteer work. She might have gained self-awareness from this reflection, but it would not give her the meaning of her volunteer experience. Neither problem-solving nor psychological analysis leads us directly to the meaning of our experience in terms of our faith in God—its theological meaning.

The discomfort of dealing with the unknown in reflection, or distress with the experiences we bring to reflection, can tempt us to turn to problem-solving or psychological analysis because these are more familiar to us than theological reflection. Both reconnect us quickly to familiar frameworks of interpretation and systems of meaning. But this rapid reconnection to the familiar can block the discovery of new meaning through the movement toward insight.

In the movement toward insight, an image that captures the central feeling of an experience is the clue to its meaning. This image invites relationship. It evokes from us an attuned subjective connection to our experience. The image helps us avoid a distanced analysis of our experience that disguises premature interpretations of it.

The image that captures our feelings in an event is a second-level metaphor or symbol. The bodily sensations that accompanied those feelings comprised a first-level or embodied symbol. As a metaphor or symbol the image is both concrete, referring to a particular event, and universal, connecting that event to human experience at a deep level. The more it captures a very particular experience, the more it invites resonance with the experiences of others. In this way an image or metaphor can convey the energy of common but very profound human experiences. Symbolizing our experience in an image intensifies and deepens that experience. It leads us on a journey into the particular that eventually unites our own concrete question to the transhistorical, transcultural questions and experiences of existence, and allows others to enter into them as well.

Noticing Images in Your Life

1. Listen to a conversation among coworkers or friends, paying attention to the images that are used. Which symbolize feelings? What feelings do they symbolize?

2. Recall your conversations during a day. Identify situations where you used images to express feelings or state the crux of a situation.

3. Recall a situation from the past week about which you have strong feelings. Reenter that experience and from within it describe your physical sensations as fully as possible until you find yourself saying "It's like . . ." The words you use to fill in the blank will be an image that captures the experience.

4. Listen to the dialogue in your favorite television show or film. Do images symbolize feelings and situations in the dialogue? How?

Insight

Considering and Questioning
Those Images May Spark Insight

Sometimes when we muse on a situation an image emerges that at once captures the essence of our conundrum and frees us from it. Such is the power of images. They can compress many

INSIGHT

aspects of a situation into an integrated, intense wholeness and at the same time open us to new angles of vision. Images help us break free of our habitual ways of interpreting our lives by impelling us to make meaning in new ways.

At other times in our ponderings, an image emerges that surprises us. We play with the image, wondering what it means, questioning how it relates to the original situation of our reflection. Often such an image pleases and perturbs us, satisfies and startles us, all at once. By so doing it demands our attention and prods our reflective process.

Images invite consideration. Their capacity to capture, intensify, and transform a situation makes them powerful. When an image grabs our attention it compels us to relate to it in an open and welcoming way. Because images can capture the crux of a situation, but do so in a way that shifts from the original narrative structure to a symbolic structure, they can spark insight. An image transports our situation and us to a new space, a new standpoint from which we can view and experience the original situation differently. By entering the space of the image we open ourselves to new insight, to new learning, to being changed, and potentially to revelation.

In the musings of our daily life our consideration of images may be random and spontaneous. We hardly may be aware that we are considering the image. At other times we may consider and question an image using a particular orientation. Perhaps we have read a book on interpreting dreams and find ourself using its questions to address our image. Or we might have taken a professional development workshop on power and communication and find ourselves approaching the image from that perspective. Considering and questioning images is a natural part of our reflective process. Our reflection becomes theological when we use questions arising from themes in our Christian heritage to explore an image that emerges from our experience.

The fruit of considering and questioning an image we call insight. Insight can come seemingly instantaneously and evoke an exclamation of "Aha!" or "I've got it!" or a shift in body sensation. Or insight can come slowly, entering our consciousness very gently. However it comes, insight may invite subtle or profound, small or large transformations of our being and actions. New information may be discovered or new perspectives gained. New possibilities may become apparent, or a cherished idea or goal elucidated or enhanced. Our own actions and beliefs may be confirmed or revealed to be in need of revision. We may become aware for the first time of what we truly believe and think.

Insight is most often stimulated by the consideration and questioning of an image. When an insight occurs, wherever in the process, it is important to capture it in word or symbol so that it is not lost. We can write it down or sketch it. Often valuable insights first occur as thoughts flitting across our consciousness. We need to take a few minutes to record them for further consideration.

Insights are an invitation to transformation. Not all will prove equally valuable or appropriate for our faithful growth at any particular time. We can be confident, however, that an important insight, one that carried a crucial invitation from God, will continue to emerge during our reflections until we respond.

Images and Insights in Your Life

1. Retrieve images that have been particularly important to you in your life. You may find them in a photograph or a

drawing or a place or a phrase from a poem, hymn, story, or musical lyrics that you have valued. How has any one of these images invited your consideration? How have you considered and questioned it in your reflection?

2. If you belong to a church, religious community, or prayer group, identify some of its central images. How does the structure of your worship invite consideration of these images?

3. Recall two significant insights that you have had in your life. How did they come to you? What feelings accompanied them? What holds these insights in your memory? Are images involved in remembering either or both of them?

Action

Insight Leads, if We Are Willing, to Action

A very lucky man describes a moment of revelation that came after he had almost burned himself to death while freebasing cocaine. While recovering in the hospital he was telling a friend how this incident had brought him to his senses, how he now saw the error of his ways, how cocaine had ruined his life. His insights were vivid and well articulated. However, his friend listened with a growing sense of unease to all of the learnings that were flowing from the man's mouth. "Yes, but what are you going to *do*, Timothy?" he asked at intervals. He knew that insight alone would not save the gentleman; a radical change in lifestyle was necessary.

Until our lives change as a result of what we have learned, insight remains incomplete. The Christian way itself is not primarily a matter of increased knowledge or understanding, but of incarnating the truth we receive so that we come to embody the love of God in the world. Then the course of our lives changes.

In the story above, the consequences of acting or not acting on the insight received are extreme—literally a matter of life or death. More often the choices that face us are less dramatic; a

ACTION

father notices that he seems a stranger among his own children; a lawyer experiences a strong desire to respond to anarticle expounding the value of pro bono work; a young woman at a church conference comes to a new sense of her vocation as a Christian in the world. For these people as for all of us, putting into practice what has been discovered is not automatic. "The road to hell is paved with good intentions" is a piece of wisdom from First World culture that describes the possibility that our insights and intentions wither away, leaving us locked into patterns of behavior that go against our better judgment.

What are we to do if new action does not spring from our insights? There are three key elements in overcoming our inertia and moving from insight to action. These elements are prayer, planning, and other people. We do not create our own insights but receive them as gifts; so also we open ourselves in prayer to receive the courage to move into new territory. Then we can pursue the trail to which our insights point us by deliberately planning some new behavior and asking the people around us for the support that we need to follow through on what we have decided.

Insight to Action in Your Life

1. Recall a time when you intended to act on insight in your life, to change your behavior in some way. Did you succeed? Did you make this change entirely on your own?

2. Recall a time in your life when you sought support from others: friends or professionals or a group to help you make a change in your life. What happened?

3. What feelings and thoughts have been involved for you in making changes in your life?

Summary

For human beings the drive for meaning is stronger than the drive for physical survival. We need to make sense of what happens to us, to clothe our existence within an interpretive pattern that reflects back to us lives of integrity, coherence, and significance. If we cannot, the will to live withers.

The deep and compelling drive for meaning motivates us to reflect. Often we are unaware of our reflective process. The movement toward insight describes what we do when we ponder and muse over events, people, and ideas. We reflect when events do not fit easily into our interpretive frameworks, the constructs we use to make meaning of our lives.

The movement toward insight is like a journey. We travel from experience through feeling to image to new ideas and awareness that can change and enrich our lives. At our most intuitive, we may not be aware of the flow of the movement. Bringing it to awareness allows our reflection to become more conscious and critical. Practicing our awareness of the movement leads to increased knowledge and more perceptive sensibilities in relation to our selves, family, community, the earth, and our religious tradition. It opens us to being more discerning of God's presence and action in our lives. Bringing the movement toward insight to awareness provides an entry into formal theological conversation.

3

Theology as a Form
of Human Reflection

Grounding Theology in Human Reflection

The movement toward insight explains how we come to new understandings in our lives. Whether we muse over events intuitively and unself-consciously or ponder situations deliberately and intently, we come to insights that invite us to fresh ways of perceiving and acting. Our musings and ponderings bring us to the meanings of our lives.

But are we all alone in this process of uncovering the meanings of our lives? Are all our insights trustworthy? How can we test our insights? How do the standpoints from which we reflect influence the meanings to which we come?

While each of us must engage in uncovering the meanings of our own lives, we need not to do so in isolation. The Christian community, past and present, offers companionship in the process of moving toward insight. Further, the rich wisdom contained in the Christian community's theological heritage offers a context within which to test, refine, and expand our insights as we carry them back into our daily lives. The Christian heritage provides a body of religious wisdom that we can incorporate into our reflection on life experiences. When we deliberately incorporate wisdom from our Christian heritage into the process of uncovering the meanings in our life experiences we are doing theological reflection.

Standpoints and Theological Reflection

The standpoint we occupy during reflection markedly influences the quality and trustworthiness of the insights that result when we bring our lives to our Christian heritage. The standpoints of certitude and self-assurance block reflection and lead to trite insights and diminished understandings. The standpoint of exploration encourages full-blown reflection and leads to surprising insights and transformative understandings.

In the standpoint of certitude we think that we already know, or easily can come to know, what our lived experience means, because we think we understand our Christian religious heritage. In this standpoint, reflection involves catching what happens to us—events, thoughts, feelings, questions—and placing them quickly into the boxes of our preestablished religious interpretive framework.

Consider again the example of Elaine:

> Elaine worked one night each week as a volunteer in a shelter for the homeless. She found herself tense and tired at the end of these sessions. As she reflected on her experience she described the tension she was feeling "like a steel rod across my shoulders." The image became a shorthand for what life was like in that situation.

If Elaine reflected on her situation from the standpoint of certitude she might continue with comments such as these:

> "Suffering is part of following Jesus; I should not mind being tense."

> "If only I had more faith, I would be able to do my volunteer work joyfully instead of ending up with a backache."

> "What is wrong with feeling tension when I am working in the homeless shelter? The place is terrible, the people are broken by personal and structural sin, why think anything else is possible?"

Notice that in each of these continuations of her reflection Elaine departs from exploring the image "a steel rod across my shoulders," which symbolizes her experience as a volunteer in the homeless shelter. Instead she moves toward fitting her experience at the shelter into her current religious interpretive framework. The statements she makes from that framework,

"Suffering is part of following Jesus," a desire to have "more faith," and that in a homeless shelter one confronts people "broken by personal and structural sin" are all true statements. The question is: Does any one statement, or all of them, occasion genuine insight for Elaine? Do the statements offer Elaine new meaning in terms of her particular experience as a volunteer in the homeless shelter? Is any one of these already known religious truths the revelation God may be offering her in her experience?

The problem with reflecting from the standpoint of certitude is that it allows in no new meanings or surprises. Nothing changes for Elaine when she reflects this way. She is not able to act differently, she does not perceive differently, there is no insight or liberation or empowerment. Reflection from the standpoint of certitude simply reinforces the way things are emotionally, politically, economically, and in every other way. This theological reflection leaves a stale taste in our mouths and a heaviness in our hearts.

Bringing the wisdom of our religious tradition into reflection done from the standpoint of self-assurance also frustrates the movement toward insight. In the standpoint of self-assurance we rely solely on our current experience and perspectives, what we think and feel now. If we refer to the wisdom of our Christian heritage we do so to reinforce what we already think, to support the agendas we already hold.

In the standpoint of self-assurance we think that we already know, or easily can come to know, what our Christian religious heritage means because we think we understand our lived experience. In this standpoint, reflection involves catching pieces of our Christian religious heritage—Scripture passages, theological themes, received traditions—and placing them quickly into the boxes of our preestablished interpretive framework.

Consider again the example of Elaine. If Elaine reflected on her situation from the standpoint of self-assurance, she might continue with comments such as these:

> "I know the shelter needs volunteers, but I do not need another burden right now. Jesus does not ask us to be masochists, so I am going to quit this volunteer work."

"The work at the shelter is overwhelming. The pain that I feel being around those broken people, some just losers, some innocent victims, is just too much for me to handle. I feel only distress when I work there. It can't be Christian service if distress is all I feel."

"I really don't like the way this work makes me feel. I need to stick with it to get the information I need for the project in my required introduction to theology course, but once that is done, I'll be gone from that place."

Notice that in each of these continuations of Elaine's reflection her own feelings and needs have become the overpowering reality that consumes her. "Steel rod across my shoulders" ceases to be the symbol or image of her situation and becomes the situation in its totality. Elaine does not explore the image or her feelings and needs for their meaning. Rather, they have become the meaning of her experience. Neither does Elaine's reflection from the standpoint of self-assurance look to the Christian religious heritage for insight into her experience. She draws on the tradition to support her preestablished understanding of her experience. "Steel rod across my shoulders" is simply the way it is.

There is no room for newness in reflection from the standpoint of self-assurance. The statements Elaine makes may be true of her experience. The work at the shelter may be a "burden," "overwhelming," "distressing," or necessary to achieve some other goal. But is this the whole truth about her experience? Do these statements of intense feeling or calculated agenda capture the full meaning of the experience "steel rod across my shoulders"? Do these statements garner insights or offer new meanings to Elaine in terms of her particular experience as a volunteer in the homeless shelter?

The problem with reflecting from the standpoint of self-assurance is that it allows in no new meanings or surprises. Nothing changes for Elaine when she reflects this way. She is not able to act differently in the situation, she does not perceive differently, there is no insight or liberation or empowerment. Theological reflection from the standpoint of self-assurance, like that from the standpoint of certitude, simply reinforces the way things are emotionally, politically, economically, and in every other way.

If we want to encounter the wisdom of our Christian heritage in a way that empowers and offers transformative insights, we must bring that heritage into our reflection from the standpoint of exploration. In this standpoint we know that coming to understand both our religious heritage and our own experience is a lifelong process of the journey of faith. In this standpoint we willingly reexperience all the dimensions of the situations on which we reflect. We enter reflection open to the possibility that our interpretive frameworks are in need of revision and will be changed by our reflection and experiences. In this standpoint we rely on the rich heritage of our Christian tradition as a primary source of wisdom. We do so expecting it to speak to our particular experience, not as application of an abstract general truth, but as a liberating word addressed directly to each of us personally.

Consider again the example of Elaine. If Elaine reflected on her situation from the standpoint of exploration, she might continue:

> "What does this image, 'steel rod across my shoulders' tell me about my experience? Steel bars are strong, capable of bearing a great load. They are also rigid rather than flexible. They are incredibly heavy, too. Is there a way for me to carry this load, to be strong without being rigid? Can I be both strong and flexible? What is the source of the rigidity in my experience at the shelter?

> The image 'steel rod across my shoulders' brings to mind Jesus' saying, 'Come to me, all you that are weary and are carrying heavy burdens, and I will give you rest. Take my yoke upon you and learn from me, for I am gentle and humble in heart, you will find rest for your souls, for my yoke is easy, and my burden is light.' (Matthew 11:28–29) I'm not sure what this Gospel passage means given the way my neck feels at the end of each session at the shelter. This week I will pray with these words of Jesus before I go to the shelter and keep them in my heart as I do my volunteer work. Pondering these words while I am at the shelter may give me a

hint. As well, this promise of Jesus may give me more inner freedom while I work there than I feel now."

Notice that Elaine's reflection from the standpoint of exploration is a process directed both to her experience and to her Christian religious heritage. There is a genuine dialogue between the two. The process is open to new insights, new understandings that can bring changed behavior and perceptions.

Genuine theological reflection takes place in the standpoint of exploration. Here it is possible to bring the wisdom of our religious heritage into our process of reflection in a way that gives us new meanings. Our definition of theological reflection assumes the standpoint of exploration:

> Theological reflection is the discipline of exploring our individual and corporate experience in conversation with the wisdom of a religious heritage. The conversation is a genuine dialogue that seeks to hear from our own beliefs, actions, and perspectives, as well as from those of the tradition. It respects the integrity of both. Theological reflection therefore may confirm, challenge, clarify, and expand how we understand our own experience and how we understand the religious tradition. The outcome is new truth and meaning for living.

In our lives we move among the standpoints of certitude, self-assurance, and exploration. In a very real sense the standpoint of exploration is a gift, a trust that God is with us and for us, even when we cannot see how. The Christian tradition calls this trust faith. We cannot will ourselves to live our entire lives within the standpoint of exploration. As we grow in faith, however, we occupy this standpoint more easily and frequently.

The spiritual life itself is a journey into the standpoint of exploration where we encounter God and ourselves. Part of the discipline of that journey is to begin to notice the standpoint we occupy when we muse or reflect. Spiritual discipline calls us to become aware of how our standpoint is influencing our experience and our reflection. Nonjudgmental awareness of the standpoint we occupy provides a better way to be prepared for God to move us in faith to the standpoint of exploration than does judging ourselves for frequently occupying the standpoints of certitude or self-assurance.

Theological Reflection

Theological reflection involves bringing our religious heritage, in this case the Christian heritage, into our reflection on experience done from the standpoint of exploration. Sometimes we do this spontaneously. For example, on a hike or during a retreat we may sense that we are touched by a transcendent dimension and so turn almost automatically to the images and concepts of the Christian tradition to interpret the experience. Or we may bring the wealth of images, themes, and values acquired by being part of the Christian community to our reflection on situations from family, work, and community life. For example, we may seek to relate to a particularly difficult coworker by reminding ourselves of Jesus' saying "Love your enemies, do good to those who hate you" (Luke 6:27).

While such spontaneous theological reflection can help us reinforce our current understandings of our experience and of our tradition, it rarely takes those understandings to a deeper level or leads to mutual criticism between experience and tradition. This is because the connection between contemporary experience and the Christian heritage is seldom obvious. Surface-level correspondences between a current experience and a piece of the tradition generally miss the more significant meanings of each. Even clumsy attempts to relate our experience and our Christian heritage, however, are signs of faithful intent.

We miss much that the tradition offers to enrich our lives and much of the revelatory power of our lived experience when we keep our theological reflection solely at the spontaneous level. We are invited as Christians to a disciplined approach to bringing our religious heritage into our reflection on life experience. A disciplined approach requires that we become more self-conscious about the reflective processes we use. At the same time, it can open new paths in our own discipleship. Disciplined reflection can deepen our understanding of our heritage and our particular calling as Christians. Moving from spontaneous forms of theological reflection to a more deliberate and disciplined form supports the journey to mature faith.

The presentation of the movement toward insight in chapter 2 made us more aware of how we reflect in our ordinary living. Expanding and refining the movement toward insight transforms it into a framework for theological reflection. A framework for theological reflection is a structure by which we can bring our religious heritage into our reflection on lived experience in a deliberate manner.

The remainder of this chapter explains theology and theological reflection by presenting a framework developed from the movement toward insight. Chapter 4 translates this theory into practical processes for theological reflection.

The movement toward insight is:

- When we enter our *experience* we encounter our *feelings*.
- When we pay attention to those *feelings*, *images* arise.
- Considering and questioning those *images* may spark insight.
- *Insight* leads, if we are willing and ready, to *action*.

By expanding and refining this movement in three ways we reach a framework for theological reflection. The three changes involve: (1) expanding the concept of experience; (2) determining on what to reflect; and, (3) deliberately incorporating a religious heritage into reflection.

Expanding on Experience for Theological Reflection

Experience includes events in which we are direct participants and events in which we are passive. Elaine's work at the homeless shelter entails her active, direct participation. Cooking dinner, visiting with family, directing a project at work, buying groceries, praying—these and more involve us directly. But events in which we have no active role are also a part of our experience. Wars and famine across the globe, successful movements for social justice such as the freeing of political prisoners and ecological disasters are part of our experience, too. They shape the context of our daily lives and we respond to them with a range of feelings and thoughts.

All events involve interaction with ourselves and the world around us. Experience is the flow of interaction between a person and all the other people, places, events, material conditions, and cultural factors that constitute that person's identity, context, and world.[1] Experience is a river in which we swim like fish in water.

Experience is massive. Undifferentiated experience is too huge for any person to comprehend at one time. No individual can be fully aware of and focus simultaneously on the entire flow of people, places, events, thoughts, feelings, material artifacts, and ideas that make up her or his experience. This is why we tend to reflect on particular or specific events when we muse in our lives, like Elaine's volunteer experience. We need to reflect on humanly manageable pieces of our experience.

In order to make all of experience manageable for reflection, theologians slow down its flow and distinguish among its aspects. They divide experience into categories called sources. The sources for theology provide stable referent points for organizing and distinguishing the full range of human experience. We can say that all of Experience, with a large "E," is divided into experiences with a small "e," which are each given a different name and together are known as sources for theology. So, all the sources for theology are part of the totality of human Experience.[2]

Action (Lived Narrative)

In the movement toward insight we tend to begin reflection by focusing on one aspect of experience, our lived narrative. This is composed of stories or events that make up our life. From a young mother:

> I was washing dishes and looking out my kitchen window at my three-year-old daughter swinging. As I observed her she stopped, frowned, ran in from the swing and threw her arms

around me and said, "Mommy, I love you" and went back outside. I smiled and began to cry.

Lived narrative includes all the actions an individual has taken, and the thoughts, feelings, and perspectives associated with those actions, even if these thoughts and feelings are not in the foreground of one's awareness. We call our life stories or lived narratives the *action source*. In the movement toward insight we begin with this source most frequently.

Tradition

Our religious tradition comprises another aspect of experience. The *tradition source* includes authoritative Scriptures, doctrinal teachings, stories of denominational heroes and heroines, saints, church history, official church documents, and the like. The New Testament Gospels are part of this source. So are stories of St. Teresa of Avila, whom we know lived, and St. Christopher, who probably is a legend. For all Christians, Scripture is central to the tradition.

Denominations differ over how much popular lore or official church teaching is included. Roman Catholicism and Anglicanism, for example, give their historic creedal statements and their robust traditions of saints and spiritual practices a certain weight of authority. By contrast, the Christian Church (Disciples of Christ), a nineteenth-century American denomination founded on the conviction, "No creed but Christ," gives little authority to historic creedal statements. The denomination's founders saw these statements too often having divided Christians and drawn them away from following Jesus. Instead the Disciples of Christ focus on the Scripture, practice being silent where Scripture is silent, and leave belief statements beyond those in Scripture up to individuals being guided by faithfulness and their own reasoning abilities.

Tradition is a special source in theological reflection. For Christians, the Christian tradition carries authority because we trust that it can relate us to God and to the wisdom of all our Christian forebears in a powerful way. For persons from other religious traditions—Buddhism, Judaism, Islam, or African, Native American, and other indigenous tribal traditions—their own religious heritage constitutes their authoritative tradition source. Among converts to Christianity both Christianity and their indigenous religious tradition may be authoritative sources for theological reflection. The same may hold true for Christians who convert to another religious tradition. Religious pluralism and interreligious dialogue may be leading us to a situation in the twenty-first century where increasing numbers of people will have multiple authoritative religious tradition sources. They will draw on all of them in their theological reflection.

Culture

A far more influential aspect of experience than we commonly imagine is culture. *Culture* is so large and dominant a source that it is most easily conceived as having three distinct but inseparable parts. The first is culture, narrowly defined. This includes the symbols, mores, assumptions, values, sciences, artifacts, and philosophies of human groups. A nation's flag, social norms against incest, notions of common sense, honoring individualism, prizing honesty in business, evolutionary theory, Michelangelo's paintings on the ceiling of the Sistine Chapel, pragmatist philosophy, and in pluralistic societies, the wisdom of religious traditions not our own are all elements of European and United States culture. Every human group, small or large, has a culture in this sense.

The second sense of culture involves the patterns of organized interaction within human groups. This includes the ways we structure our economic interactions, our political system, our educational system, law, and family; the ways we act out being mothers, fathers, siblings, friends, employees, and community leaders. This second element of culture is called social structure.

Social structure, invisible and taken for granted when it works for most people, shapes profoundly how we see and think about the world. For example, the civil rights movement of the 1950s and 1960s faced massive, violent opposition because it sought to change racist social structures that most people in the United States assumed were simply the way reality was. During the 1960s and 1970s opposition to the war in Vietnam brought to awareness the social structure of draft-based compulsory military service for healthy males. This structure was eventually changed. Today in the United States some states organize their welfare systems to penalize recipients in order to discourage people from using these services. The structure is based on a cultural assumption, namely, that there exists a large population of "undeserving poor," people who are on welfare because they are too lazy to work.

We often do not think about social structures precisely because they structure—give order to—our reality. They are especially invisible when they reflect the commonly held values and assumptions that we described as the first element of culture. Social structures come to our awareness when we begin to realize that they do not embody the values we say we hold or when we recognize the ways in which these structured relationships positively militate against our best values and self-understandings.

A form of theological reflection that begins by focusing primarily on social structures often is called *social analysis.* This form of theological reflection teaches people how to notice and describe the social structures that shape their daily lives and how to analyze them in light of the gospel message. Social analysis is uncomfortable and surprising for many middle-class people in the United States because this culture highlights and values individual action and initiative. Middle-class culture tends not to notice the interrelatedness of people in social structures. (Resources on social analysis are listed in the Resources for Theological Reflection.)

The third element of culture, one to which Christians are only now beginning to turn their attention, is the physical environment. Issues of population, garbage, deadly industrial and nuclear wastes, air quality, and preservation of ancient forests are forcing us all to think more about the ecological context of our lives, about the earth and air and water. Scientific data supporting the theory that the earth itself is a living organism requires much more sustained reflection on ecological issues by all religious people.

Positions

Besides action (lived narrative), tradition (the religious wisdom that we accept as authoritative), and culture (ideas, social structures, ecological environment), every person harbors *positions,* the fourth aspect of experience. Position refers to the attitudes, opinions, beliefs, and convictions that one holds and is willing to defend in argument. "A violent environment during childhood cripples an individual," "A mother's place is in the home," "People are responsible for their actions," "Changing the pattern of worship is always bad," and, "The United States should be the peacekeeper of the world," are examples of position statements that an individual might hold. Position statements often involve our understandings of roles and values associated with society, politics, religion, and economics.

When we articulate a current interpretation of an event in our lives or an interpretation of something in our culture, or our tradition, we are articulating our positions. For example, the statements, "My recent illness brought me closer to God," "The violence in our society has multiple causes," or "The Roman Catholic Church's teachings on birth control are problematic," all constitute interpretations that are positions. Positions are the statements of the meaning we have made, our interpretation of life.

The more self-consciously and purposively reflective we become, the more aware we become of the role positions play within our individual experience. Positions seem almost to have a life of their own. Learning to identify and to revise our positions constitutes an important part of growing in faith, because our positions either can keep us from seeing God's activity in our lives or make it more obvious to us. Positions have a life of their own.

Action (lived narrative), tradition, culture, and positions designate the four sources for theology. These four together are aspects of Experience: the flow of interaction between an individual and the people, places, events, material conditions, and cultural factors that make up that person's identity, context, and world. The four sources are ways to separate out elements of that flow in order to make reflection possible.

In order to reflect, the flow of experience must be stopped. We cannot reflect on experience in its entirety. We need manageable pieces of experience in order to reflect, so we take a single event or issue and focus on that for reflection. We freeze Experience in a moment of time and separate it into aspects or sources.

The following description, illustrated on page 60, gives a visual representation of Experience and the sources for reflection.

Experience is the flowing river of interactions with people, places, events, and other factors that make up our lives. Experience always has inner and outer dimensions and always is greater than we can comprehend at any given moment.

In the river is a prism contained in a sphere. Each point on the prism is a source for theological reflection. Sources are aspects of Experience. The prism represents the dynamic relationship among the sources. Even though we separate Experience into aspects to make reflection possible, the meaning of any particular event is revealed only when we attend to these aspects or sources and their mutual relationships.

The prism is contained within a sphere to remind us that in order to reflect we must freeze the flow of Experience and focus on a smaller, concrete event or situation. The sphere represents the river of Experience frozen at an instant in time.

When we reflect, we stop the flow of interaction with our contexts, freeze it in time by focusing on one particular event or situation, and place a structure on it by thinking of the event in terms of sources. This process allows us to begin to discover the fuller meaning of a particular event, especially its meaning in light of the Christian heritage. It helps us to slow down our habitual meaning-making processes, so that we can look more closely at a situation and at how we are making meaning of it.

Sources for theology are constructs we put on experience to organize it. Other ways of dividing the flow of Experience are possible and other names for sources can be used. The volumes by Whitehead and Whitehead and Wingeier listed in the Resources for Theological Reflection name sources differently.

We have elaborated our definition of experience from the movement toward insight in terms of sources for theological reflection. This elaboration offers many more starting points for reflection.

In theological reflection we identify and select data from one of the sources, or aspects of Experience, to be the beginning point of our reflection. Having begun, however, we confront an-

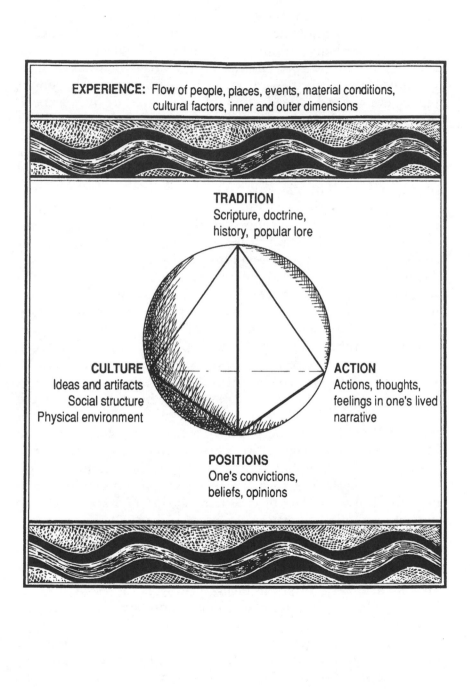

EXPERIENCE: Flow of people, places, events, material conditions, cultural factors, inner and outer dimensions

TRADITION
Scripture, doctrine, history, popular lore

CULTURE
Ideas and artifacts
Social structure
Physical environment

ACTION
Actions, thoughts, feelings in one's lived narrative

POSITIONS
One's convictions, beliefs, opinions

other question: On what will we reflect in a particular experience? How do we enter that experience to begin to discern its meaning?

Naming the Significant Issue
of an Experience for Reflection

In the second part of movement toward insight we *pay attention to our feelings and images arise.* The feeling/image combination symbolizes the significant issue in the experience we bring to reflection. In the example of Elaine, "a steel rod across my shoulders" captures the heart of her experience as a volunteer in the shelter for the homeless. Such a combination of feeling/image allows us to reflect on the central issue in an event even before we have precise language for stating it conceptually.

In theological reflection we call the significant issue of an event brought for reflection the *heart of the matter.* The phrase refers to the central question, tension, issue, theme, problem, or wonderment of an experience. Why do innocent children suffer? How can I resolve my desire to be a good mother and my desire to succeed in my chosen career? How do I live with a drug-dependent spouse without becoming codependent? Why is it that toxic waste incinerators are placed disproportionately in poor neighborhoods? What is the source of the beauty of this mountain? Whatever the heart of the matter is, it invites exploration and interpretation.

The strategy from the movement toward insight for stating the heart of the matter is to let our experience give us its key feelings that lead us to an image. For example,

> Alice escaped to the mountains for two days in January with a good friend from college years. When she returned she was refreshed and smiling. In her reflection on the event she says, "The time with my friend, Julia, was like violets pushing up through the snow for me."

This simple image articulates the heart of the matter of Alice's experience in symbolic form. Expressing the heart of the matter of an experience in an image constitutes the most intuitive and relational way of stating the significant issue of an experience.

The feeling/image strategy works well, too, in theological reflection. Sometimes, however, we need other ways to articulate the significant content of an event brought for reflection. The crux of the experience may be expressed in a sentence identifying a tension or issue or problem. For example,

> "I want to live out my vocational call to matrimony *and* I want to maintain my emotional health in the face of my spouse's drug addiction."

> "I want to serve the Catholic Church as a priest *and* I am a woman."

> "I want to care for the environment *and* I want to buy a home that will require me to commute to work alone."

The first statement captures the tension or issue that a Christian committed to her or his marriage and facing a drug-addicted spouse might experience. The second expresses the tension female members of the Catholic Church endure when they experience a call to priesthood. The third statement reveals the inner tension of wanting to be ecologically responsible and wanting to fulfill one's own desires. All three statements, however, capture the heart of the matter of an experience in its central tension.

Learning to identify the heart of the matter or the epicenters of an event and to articulate them for theological reflection is an artful process. Practicing careful nonjudgmental description of experience is a first step. Often in the telling of the event we will find ourselves led to the heart of the matter.

We may have to discern among several possible elements in an event, knowing that we cannot reflect on all of them at once. If an event contains several points for reflection then it can be the focus of reflection more than once. Most of our individual and corporate experience is far richer than we know.

However we articulate the heart of the matter for theological reflection, we want to state the significant aspect of the particular experience succinctly enough for reflection to be focused. "A steel rod across my shoulders," "Violets pushing up through the snow," "I want to be ecologically responsible and I want to purchase a home that will require me to commute to work by myself," and the other examples in this chapter succinctly focus attention for reflection. Each contains the core of an experience.

We also want to articulate the crux of an experience for theological reflection in a way that carries the affective energy of the situation. This affective energy is important because it carries our whole or embodied response to a situation. Gentle, nonjudgmental narration of the event allows this energy to come through. Look again at the young mother's brief story:

> I was washing dishes and looking out my kitchen window at my three-year-old daughter swinging. As I observed her she stopped, frowned, ran in from the swing and threw her arms around me and said, "Mommy, I love you" and went back outside. I smiled and began to cry.

Notice that her description is simple but clear. It tells "who" did "what," "when," "where," and "how." It contains no judgments, such as "I know this is silly but," "I really don't understand why I began to cry, there must be something wrong with me," "I know I spent too much time just watching my daughter." The description gently and nonjudgmentally reconstructs the event, both its inner and outer dimensions.

Such gentle, nonjudgmental description helps evoke an apt image or statement that enables the heart of the matter to emerge. The image or statement will contain the affective energy of the original experience. For the young mother the image, "A butterfly emerging from its cocoon" and the statement, "I was embraced by unconditional love," captured the crux of her experience.

Once we have focused on material from one of the sources and have determined the heart of the matter, the epicenter of the situation, we want to bring that to our religious heritage. This leads to the third point where we change the movement toward insight—this time deliberately to incorporate our religious heritage into our reflection.

Putting the Heart of the Matter in Conversation with Wisdom of the Christian Heritage

In theological reflection we bring experience to our Christian heritage so that we can receive wisdom and the power of our faithfulness can be released. This intent gives a deliberate direction to our reflection. We want to develop and test our insights in relation to the wisdom of our foremothers and forefathers in faith. We want to create a context of dialogue between our own beliefs, actions, and perspectives in an event and those of our religious tradition.

For theological reflection we want to bring our experience to the tradition so that a surprising encounter—newness—can emerge. The image of conversation expresses this. The Christian heritage influences our lives most vitally when it surprises us. Indeed, the tradition cannot speak to us unless we are willing for what is familiar to become unfamiliar. If we always know what the tradition says, we are acting from the standpoint of certitude and will read our current positions onto the tradition rather than hear God's Word.

Scripture, official church teaching, popular lore, historical incidents, all these and more from the heritage can shed new light and reveal richer meanings in our living. The temptation, however, is to take our experience to the tradition in a way that simply reinforces whatever preliminary, or prior, interpretation of the event we have already.

To put it another way, our habitual meaning-making processes do not want to be upset by new knowledge or insight. Change is uncomfortable. If we learn something new from the Christian heritage, we may have to revise our interpretive frameworks or our positions and learn new ways of making meaning and of behaving. Similarly, our experience may help us to see new truths or depth in the tradition that again will require us to change our theological positions.

In genuine conversation among persons we bracket or set aside our fears, pride, and scrupulosity and let the subject matter of the conversation carry us along to new understanding. Genuine conversations are a reciprocal movement full of surprise, sometimes delightful, sometimes sobering. This is what we aim for when we put the heart of the matter, or the most energy-filled point of an event, into conversation with the wisdom of the Christian heritage.

The technical name for building a context in which conversation between our experience and the wisdom of our religious heritage can take place is *correlation*. Think of it as corelating, bringing two things together and relating them to each other.

As we are using it, correlation involves two parts. First we explore the heart of the matter of the experience brought to reflection using questions drawn from the central themes of our Christian heritage. These questions direct us to the theological or religious meaning of our experience. For example, Elaine's experience in the homeless shelter, captured in the image, "a steel rod across my shoulders," might be explored with one or more of the following questions:

> What is existence like with a steel rod across one's shoulders?
>
> What is negative about carrying a steel rod across one's shoulders?
>
> Is anything life-giving about carrying a steel rod across one's shoulders?
>
> What might make it better to carry a steel rod across one's shoulders?

These four questions are based respectively in the Christian themes of creation, sin, grace, and salvation. The questions do not use these theological code words. Rather, they ask of Elaine's experience, captured in the image, the question to which each of these Christian themes is an answer. The theme of creation describes reality or existence; sin explains the negativity in our lives; grace describes what empowers us in the direction of life; and salvation names the healing and renewal that we experience. This process of reflecting on our experience using questions developed from classic Christian themes is described more fully in chapter 6.[3]

The second part of correlation involves including material from the tradition source in our reflection whenever we begin a reflection from the sources of action, culture, or positions. We bring in material from the tradition to help in our consideration of the heart of the matter. In the example of Elaine, she found herself drawn to material from the tradition source when she said that her image, "a steel rod across my shoulders," reminded her of Jesus' words, "My yoke is easy, and my burden light." To continue our example of correlation, we would explore this Scripture passage with the same questions built from Christian themes that we used to explore Elaine's experience. So, we might ask one or more of the following questions:

> What is existence like, what kind of place is the world where a "yoke is easy" and a "burden light"?
>
> How does this image of an easy yoke and light burden speak to the negative of a steel rod across the shoulders?
>
> What is life-giving or encouraging in this image for one carrying a steel rod across her or his shoulders?
>
> What does this passage suggest is healing about carrying a steel rod across one's shoulders?

The correlation, the dialogue between Elaine's experience and the tradition, would be continued by her comparing, contrasting, and exploring the answers to one or more of these questions addressed both to her experience and to the Scripture passage. From that genuinely open dialogue insights and new meanings for her life could emerge.

Gathering the Fruit of Our Reflection

Theological reflection, the conversation between experience and our Christian heritage, is like all conversations: it ends. The pressures of work and family and the need to eat and sleep impinge. Sometimes we remember vividly for a long time a truth that came to us in the conversation. Other times we may write a new insight in our journal or diary. And we may find ourselves deliberately acting in new ways as a consequence of the conversation.

Theological reflection involves a deliberate effort to identify an idea, a call to action, an image for meditation, an issue for prayer, a question for further study, or another element from the conversation between the heart of the matter and the wisdom of the Christian heritage whose significance compels us. The truth or meaning is not always something new. It can be a deepening confirmation of a truth we have long accepted. It can be a different perspective that sheds light on a complex of feelings or behaviors with which we struggle. It can be a shift in attitude or emotion that frees us to live with a different tone or quality. It can be an intense insight that leaves us in a new world, a place far more textured and rich than we ever noticed before.

The life of faith is rarely a matter of surface changes. The truth or meaning we garner from theological reflection may take root slowly and cause surprising changes. These changes occur in our perceptions and attitudes, in the way we relate to all of life. The changes can also happen in particular things we think and do.

Articulating what we take away from reflection is crucial to growing in the life of faith. Unless we write, sculpt, or in other ways embody our insights we are likely to forget them as our habitual meaning-making processes lull us back into our familiar ways of living.

Changes in perception and attitude are important for understanding the life of faith. The life of faith is not about signing on to a list of propositional statements that we repeat in a way that justifies our existence or makes us more righteous than others, or guarantees a smooth contractual relationship with God. Rather, the life of faith is about embarking on a journey into intensification, a journey into our own particular life in all its finitude with our desire to experience the infinite in it. When we live our own lives completely we reach a point where we gain a sense for the fundamental questions and feelings common to us all.[4] At this point we can receive insight and gain understanding. And we are made more free to exercise the gift of compassion, for ourselves and for others.

Genuine insight quiets our fears and dissolves the judgments that we use to separate ourselves from others and to make ourselves righteous or condemn ourselves. Genuine insights allow us to see reality, including ourselves, more truly, to be more acutely aware of God's grace within us and among us. When we see and feel God's power more clearly, compassion, the ability to feel with others, is released. We reflect theologically because it changes us. It allows us to perceive and act differently in our daily lives.

When the insight from our reflection leads to new action, we move again into experiences that provide new events for reflection. We are brought to the beginning point of reflection again.

Neither the movement toward insight nor theological reflection is a process we move through only once and then are finished. Reflection proceeds more like a directional spiral, a gyre, as in a dance, which allows backward and forward movement within a larger trajectory.

A Framework for Theological Reflection

We have made three changes in the movement toward insight in order to create a framework for deliberately connecting our reflection on life to our religious heritage; in our case, the Christian heritage. First, we expanded our concept of experience, introducing the notion of theological sources as a way of organizing and managing the flow of experience for reflection. Second, we explored how to determine on what to reflect in an event selected for reflection from one of the sources. Third, we looked at how we can incorporate our religious heritage into our reflection deliberately by structuring a correlation. Correlation involves bringing in material from the tradition source to all our reflections and using questions drawn from classic Christian themes to explore the material from the sources.

With these three alterations the movement toward insight provides the basis for a framework for theological reflection. The framework for theological reflection can be summarized this way:

1. **Focusing on** some aspect of **experience** (sources are aspects of experience)

2. **Describing that experience** to identify the **heart of the matter**

3. Exploring the Heart of the Matter **in conversation with the wisdom of the Christian heritage** (includes questions from Christian themes and material from the tradition source)

4. Identifying from this conversation **new truths and meanings** for living

All processes for theological reflection contain these four elements. They are grounded in the movement toward insight and create a deliberate bridge or correlation between the tradition source and the other sources for theology.

Structured processes for theological reflection that we can learn and employ regularly we call methods of reflection. Particular methods of reflection vary depending on their context and purpose. All methods, however, share the common fundamental elements in the framework for theological reflection. The framework provides a general pattern for thinking about theological reflection. It is a map that can guide us. It can help us find our way through the reflective process used in books of theology or sermons or retreats. It also can be used as a guide when designing methods of theological reflection.

Experiencing Theological Reflection

The following process of theological reflection follows the movement toward insight closely. Doing this reflection will help concretize the relationship between the movement and the framework for theological reflection presented in this chapter.

Do this reflection when you are calm, have uninterrupted time, and are in a quiet place. Do not worry about doing it correctly or about coming up with the proper answers. Trust your own reflective abilities.

0. You will begin this reflection by quietly contemplating a question (see step 1) until an incident, a story from your life in which you were actively involved, comes to mind. You will narrate this event by stating *who*, including your-

self, was involved, *what* was done, *where* the action occurred, *how* it occurred, and its quality. When you write your narrative in response to the question, remember that you want the event, not your interpretation of it. If you find yourself responding to the question by writing something that begins with "because" or "I think," stop. That approach yields a statement of your interpretation of the event. It does not yield a slice of your lived narrative. You want to answer the question with a narrative from your life experience.

1. Sit with the following question until an incident from your life that embodies your answer to it comes to mind: Why do you follow Jesus?

2. Identify the one or two key feelings in your narrative. Let those feelings sink into your body and breathe slowly until an image emerges. If no image emerges, use the key feeling as your image.

3. Answer these two questions: What does your image suggest about God's purposes for the world? What does your image suggest about your place in realizing God's purposes for the world? (You may want to construct a dialogue with your image and let it answer the questions for you in a conversation. You can do this by writing the conversation in the form of a script with the image and you as the characters. Alternatively, let a significant figure from your life, someone you considered wise, help you find what the image says to you about these questions.)

4. Once you have answered the two questions, sit quietly with your image again. What story, passage, or theme from Scripture, church history, popular Christian lore, or theology arises for you? Brainstorm a list. Do not ponder it, let them arise from within you and do not be concerned about how your image and the item from tradition fit together.

5. Pick one of the items that arose from tradition. If a Scripture passage came to you, take a Bible and read the passage. Then answer these questions: What does this piece of tradition say about God's purposes for the world? What

does this piece of tradition suggest about your part in realizing God's purposes for the world? Write out your answers and again do not think about it, let what comes, emerge.

6. Compare your answers to the two questions from your image and from the tradition. Are there similarities? What are they? Are there differences? What are they? Is there something significant in the contrast? Is there a theme that runs through the answers? Is there something that strikes you in all of this? Is there a question or idea that you want to consider further? You may want to write your musings on these questions as they come to you. (Our ordinary processes for making meaning often resist noticing and incorporating new things.)

7. How does the conversation between answers from your image and from the tradition strike you? What is developing through the conversation between the answers from your image and the answers from the tradition? Is a belief (perhaps one about discipleship) being confirmed or challenged or extended or deepened? Does what emerges lead you to see the original situation that you narrated differently? Are you being called to any particular action—prayer, further reflection, study, a behavior shift in your daily life? Write down your statement of the truth or meaning that has emerged for you from this reflection.

Pause between doing the reflection and continuing with the next section of the chapter. A break makes it easier to shift from employing the perceptive and reflective skills used for doing reflection to those needed to consider methods of reflection.

If you are more interested in doing reflection than in learning about how to do it, you may want to continue with the summary of this chapter and then move on to chapter 4.

Bridging from the Movement Toward Insight to Theological Reflection

The following chart compares this process of theological reflection and the movement toward insight:

Movement Toward Insight	*Reflection on Following Jesus*
	Retrieve experience in response to question
Enter experience, encounter feelings	Narrate experience, encounter feelings
Attend to feelings, image emerges	Identify key feelings, let image emerge
Consider and question image	Explore image with questions about God's purposes for the world and your place in those
	Image evokes resources from tradition
	Explore resource from tradition with questions about God's purposes and your part in realizing God's purposes
Insight may emerge	Compare answers to the questions from image and tradition. Identify and develop what emerges and how it challenges understandings
Insight leads to new action	Identify any action to which you are called

Using this chart as a reference, consider those elements that make the reflective process explicitly theological. First, the question used to direct our attention to a piece of our lived narrative from the action source focuses on a Christian theme, discipleship. Not all theological reflection, however, begins with a question that focuses on religious dimensions of our experience. Even if we always began with a religious experience, in the movement toward insight we could explore the event in other than theological ways. For example, we might do a psychological exploration of the event by asking what the narrative reveals about the human need for vision and ideals in order to live creatively.

Second, the questions for considering the key feeling or image from the narrative make this reflection theological. These questions explore the image, a symbol for our experience, in terms of two Christian themes: Providence—God's purposes for creation; and vocation—our place in realizing God's purposes for creation. Using questions grounded in classic Christian themes to consider and question the key feeling or image from a narrative turns the movement toward insight into a form of theological reflection.

Third, the reflection process builds an explicit bridge from an experience to the tradition. This bridging involves two parts. First, we let the key feeling or image take us to our Christian heritage, brainstorm resources from it, and then select an item for further exploration. Second, we explore the material from the tradition source using the same questions employed to explore the key feeling or image from the narrative.

The chart illustrates how this process for theological reflection includes all the elements of the movement toward insight. It highlights those elements of the movement that are specified in a particular way by the framework for theological reflection. Finally, it makes clear what the framework adds to the movement to make theological reflection possible.

Summary

All adult human beings who continue to grow and mature reflect and come to new insights and perspectives on their lives. Christians aim to discover the meaning of the events of their own lives and the events of their world in terms of their Christian religious heritage. When we connect our reflection on our lived experiences to our religious heritage we are moving our reflection in a theological direction. From what standpoint we reflect—certitude, self-assurance, exploration—influences the quality and trustworthiness of the insights we gain from our reflection. Today adult Christians need to connect reflection on their lives to their Christian heritage in a disciplined manner.

Christian theological reflection is grounded in the movement toward insight, the basic human reflective process. What theological reflection adds is a deliberate way of dividing experience into its aspects or sources and a deliberate bridging between tradition and the other sources that comprise our experience.

When we develop our awareness about theological reflection we are not beginning an alien activity. Rather, we are developing and refining, in light of our faith commitment, a reflective process that is deeply ingrained in us as human beings.

The following chart shows the complementarity between the movement toward insight and the framework for theological reflection presented in this chapter.

Movement	*Framework*
1. When we enter our **experience,** we encounter our **feelings.**	1. Focusing on some aspect of **experience.**
2. When we pay attention to those **feelings, images** arise.	2. Describing that experience to identify the **heart of the matter.**
3. Considering and questioning those **images** may spark **insight.**	3. Exploring the heart of the matter **in conversation with the wisdom of the Christian heritage.**
4. **Insight** leads, if we are willing and ready, to **action.**	4. Identifying from this conversation **new truths and meanings** for living.

The movement toward insight and the framework for theological reflection are very similar. The key difference lies in the third part, specifically in how the heart of the matter or the focal point from experience is considered. In the movement toward insight the image that symbolizes that point can be considered in a range of ways, drawing on the resources of a variety of disciplines, for example, sociology, psychology, or political science. In the framework for theological reflection the heart of the matter is considered in light of and drawing on resources from the Christian heritage.

The framework for theological reflection provides a foundation for our own theological reflection. This framework helps us to understand how the theology we encounter in liturgical, spiritual, or educational settings is the fruit of a human reflective process. As well, it provides broad guidelines for developing processes to enter into theological reflection on our own or in group settings.

4

Personal Theological Reflection

Making Theological Reflection
Our Own Practice

Theological reflection enriches and challenges us on our journeys in faith. It invites us to discern God's presence in the midst of our lives and to move deeply into the world and not away from it. The invitation to theological reflection should not be taken lightly for while full of promise, it requires much of those who accept.

Honesty

Honesty is the most important requirement for theological reflection. Honesty is essential because the first step in theological reflection is to look at our experience without illusion or self-deception, something human beings are reluctant to do. It is hard to learn to notice and describe our experience.

Our reluctance to notice our experience is part of the heritage of original sin, that primordial flawedness in human beings that leaves us anxious and fearful about our existence. If we describe something that has happened to us, describe it honestly, we reenter the situation and reexperience the thoughts, feelings, and physical sensations that were part of it. The more deeply we plumb the situation again, the more vulnerable we become because our exploration exposes our cherished beliefs and interpretive frameworks to critique and revision.

To travel the path of remembering and reentering our experience requires that we give up the rationalizations and self-justifications that we carry as armor. To travel this path is to enter what David Tracy calls the "journey of intensification" of experience, "a journey which most of us fear yet desire, shun yet demand."[1] Artists, heroes, and saints give us clues about what it means to desire the infinite as we travel the journey of human finitude. Doing so fully awake and aware is the journey that transforms our lives. It is the journey that leads us to a sense of the central questions and feelings that move all of us; it leads us to the Mystery that is the context of our lives.

Theological reflection invites and requires us to undertake the journey of intensification. If we overcome our fear and ambivalence toward looking at our experience and undertake the journey, if we describe and reenter our experience, we find that our lives are a treasure. For it is precisely our experience, our lives, that carry the questions that we cannot yet speak and the clues to the answers we do not yet know that we know. These fundamental questions arise from the human heart and are funded by the instinct for meaning. They ground theological reflection.

We and our Christian communities need to recognize and honor the honesty we exhibit when we reflect on our lives. We often do not recognize this honesty in ourselves or acknowledge the courage it requires. But our honesty demands recognition and is worthy to be strengthened in a supportive community of trust where real conversation can happen.

Time

It takes time to do theological reflection. Such an artful practice requires learning and refining until it seeps into our being. A disciplined reflective habit of mind and heart must penetrate our being so that it becomes part of our identity and action. The art of theological reflection is best learned and practiced in a group over an extended period of time. If a group is not possible, individuals can learn the practice of theological reflection using the resources in this book. Either in a group or on our own, regular practice over time is necessary so that the process can become part of our being and the disciplined habit of reflection can be absorbed.

We emphasize the time commitment because we live in a culture where people desire quick solutions and fast changes. Learning to reflect theologically and to incorporate reflection into our faith practice takes time, much like learning ballet or the flute. The process may seem easy, then clumsy, then frustrating, then exciting, and then comforting as it becomes a trusted resource on our faith journey.

Study, Prayer, People Skills

Theological reflection needs to be grounded in study, prayer, and interpersonal skills. First, study. When we make theological reflection part of our practice, whether individually or corporately, we need to be studying our Christian heritage in some way. Without study of Scripture, church history, or our religious heritage in some form, theological reflection rarely can deepen beyond the level of knowledge at which the individual or group begins. The reflection will not be able to move beyond what we already know. Without a continually deepening reappropriation of the tradition our theological reflection will grow stale and lifeless.

Second, theological reflection should be rooted in personal and communal prayer. A faith community that cherishes its tradition and is enriched by it sustains the practice of theological reflection. Both worship and prayer nurture and support individual and corporate openness, trust, and courage. Both are needed if we are to relate honestly to our experience, one another, and God. Both are needed if we are to experience significant insights and invitations to growth.

Finally, theological reflection presumes basic interpersonal skills. Part of being able to reflect is to learn to say "I," to speak what we mean, to listen, to clarify, to engage in conflict. Our culture provides few opportunities for us to develop these skills. Yet, developing adult communication skills is essential for the Christian community's faithfulness and effectiveness.

Authentic theological reflection, then, does not draw us into an individualized and private relationship to God and our Christian heritage. It does not allow us to use our religion to avoid ordinary life. On the contrary, authentic theological reflection draws us into our ordinary lives, with all their uniqueness, all their limits, all their richness. Only here, in the midst of our living, do we encounter the living God.

Guidelines for Individual Theological Reflection

We may choose to do theological reflection regularly during set periods of time such as a liturgical season like Lent or Advent, or around a particular life transition, or while we are working on an especially challenging project. We may want to make theological reflection a constant part of our practice throughout the year. Or we may choose to reflect theologically when we find ourselves drawn to do so.

To begin to make theological reflection part of our personal practice we must use processes for theological reflection regularly for some period of time. We need to use a process repeatedly so that its flow seeps into our being and becomes a habit of faith.

At first doing theological reflection may seem awkward. It requires that we pay attention to reflective movements that we have done unconsciously until now. By practicing processes of theological reflection we can develop our skill and comfort with it. We can become more aware also of how we reflect and make meaning of all of our lives. With practice theological reflection becomes a trusted resource for the journey of faith. Some general guidelines can assist in incorporating theological reflection into personal faith practice.

Our Attitude Toward Theological Reflection

First, we need to notice how we approach the reflective process. We want to be gentle with ourselves and our reflective process. If we approach theological reflection determined to "do the steps correctly," or "get the big insight at the end," or "solve this problem once and for all," we will short-circuit the process before we even begin.

Theological reflection is a process that works on us at a variety of levels. Often insights and shifts in sensibilities happen deep within, below our immediate consciousness. Expecting a "quick fix" or "immediate solution" to whatever situation we bring to reflection derails the reflective process and cuts us off from the deeper wisdom and growth that it offers.

We want to develop the practice of theological reflection trusting that it can attune us more acutely to the movement of God's spirit in our lives and help us to hear God's Word more fully and deeply in our Christian heritage. A trusting approach does not demand immediate results. The process of discovering the richest and truest meaning of our lives and our heritage is a gradual one.

Giving Shape and Form to Our Reflection

Regardless of the particular reflective process we use, we must give shape and form to the feelings, images, insights, and musings that come to us during reflection. We can write or draw them in a journal, verbalize them in a prayer, sculpt them in clay, or express them in dance. We can use whatever medium is comfortable and effective, but in some way we must exteriorize our reflection, move it out of the realm of thoughts.

Exteriorizing helps us to remember and absorb the fruits of our reflection. It allows us to make subtle changes in our interpretive framework and to develop more faithful strategies for making meaning of our experience.

Identifying the Heart of the Matter for Reflection

Perhaps the most challenging skill to learn when we begin doing theological reflection is how to identify the heart of the matter of a situation we bring to reflection. The heart of the matter is the focal point for our reflection, the very center of the event.

Practicing the nonjudgmental narration of our experience provides the beginning step to identifying and articulating the heart of the matter. Writing a descriptive narrative of the event we bring for reflection helps us notice our judgments in a situation and let go of them for the sake of reflection. The descriptions of incidents by Elaine, Alice, and the young mother in chapter 3 are examples of nonjudgmental narration of experience.

When writing and then rereading our narrative, we may notice one or more places in it that have an energized quality different from that of the remaining action in the narrative. An energized quality should not be confused with agitation. Sometimes that energized quality is marked by visible adrenalin, but at other times the energy's presence is contained in depth and quiet. Paying attention to the quality of energy in our narratives, and in ourselves as we write or read them over, helps us to find the place in our experience that is saturated with potential revelation.

Paying attention to our feelings in a narrative helps us to identify the central aspect of our experience for reflection. Shifts in our feelings are part of the shifts in action in a narrative. We do not want to remain caught, pleasantly or unpleasantly, in the feelings of a particular situation as we narrate it. We do want to attend to our feelings in order to begin to discern the meaning they embody. We want to allow our feelings to be what they are. We are not to judge them. We want to be open to the image that they offer.

At times our narrative may have only one focal point for reflection. At other times a narrative may contain several. In the latter case we must choose one of them to be the heart of the matter for a reflection. We can always return to an event for further reflection.

We want to articulate the focal point for reflection in a way that contains the affective energy of the original situation. This keeps us connected to the holistic energy of the event. At the same time we want to state the heart of the matter in a way that separates us slightly from the intense immediacy of the feelings in the event. This slight separation provides us with a different angle on the situation. We want these two qualities to characterize our statement of the heart of the matter whether we articulate it in an image or in a sentence.

In the example of Elaine from chapter 3, the image "a steel rod across my shoulders" captured the affective energy of the situation but separated her from the event slightly. For Alice, the statement "The time with my friend, Julia, was like 'violets push-ing up through the snow' for me" did the same. And for the young mother, the image, "a butterfly emerging from its co-coon," did the same. Also the statement she used "I was em-braced by unconditional love" captured the energy and provided slight separation to make reflection possible.

Rhythm of Reflection

Sometimes in theological reflection we find ourselves drawn to stop and linger at a point in the process. Perhaps the image in which we have captured the heart of the matter is particularly powerful and leads us into extended prayer or into parts of our own life story to which we have not attended before. Perhaps we find the image resonating with a piece of the tradition that we want to investigate through study. Such pauses to expand a step in the process of theological reflection can deepen the quality of our reflection. We must remember to bring the pause to closure and move on to complete the process. Knowledge and insights are not intellectual toys for play; they are gifts to be incorporated into our daily living.

Gathering Our Reflection

When incorporating theological reflection into our faith practice it is valuable to keep a journal of theological reflections and musings and to review it periodically. Are there images, themes, or pieces of the tradition that recur frequently? Do they invite us to particular prayer or study? Do they reveal the central tenets of our particular theological vision? Periodically we should write out our theological vision.

It is good to share insights and intentions arising from individ-ual theological reflection with a spiritual friend or guide or with a faith-sharing group where possible and appropriate. The jour-ney of faith is not an isolated journey and companions can enrich reflection as well as support us as we try new ways of living out our faith in the world. Being part of a theological reflection group is an excellent way to help make the effort a richly pro-ductive part of our faith life.

Fundamental Guideline

Above all, we want to approach our own experience and theological reflection from the standpoint of exploration. Our purpose in doing theological reflection is to be open to God's Word as it speaks to us in our experience and our Christian heritage. The standpoint of exploration allows us to receive the surprising gifts that God's Word offers.

Acting on Insights

A crucial question for us as we put our experience into conversation with the wisdom of our Christian heritage is: How does such reflection change our lives?

The discipline of regular theological reflection changes us in subtle and not so subtle ways. It may lead us to become more gentle and less judgmental in relating to those we know and those we do not know. We may find ourselves bidden to share more of our time or monetary resources with persons in need. We may become engaged in issues of social justice in our community, as advocates for the homeless, for battered women, for refugees, for children, or for persons suffering from AIDS or cancer.

Regular theological reflection forms us. In the language of the Christian tradition, it helps us be transformed by the renewal of our minds so that we can discern God's will (Rom. 12:2). Our attitudes, perceptions, and behaviors are transformed.

Sometimes a single reflection or a series of reflections results in insights that lead us to take specific actions. When reflection results in our choosing new behavior, the temptation is to go it alone, to try to change ourselves by ourselves. In fact, we need the resources that our Christian tradition offers us in order to make lasting changes: prayer, planning, and people.

Prayer

Jesus began his active ministry with a time of retreat and fasting in the desert; he prayed on the cross and continued praying with and for his followers after the resurrection. In the midst of teaching and healing Jesus would get up "a great while before dawn" to pray. As we reflect theologically as part of our intention to direct our own lives to follow where Jesus leads, times of prayer are essential. When our lives are rooted in prayer, the actions we take can become an expression of God's love for us and our response to that love.

Insight comes to us as a gift, so it is appropriate to express our gratitude, even for the insights that make us uncomfortable. Within the framework of our Christian heritage, we are encouraged to offer prayers of thanksgiving as we open our eyes each morning to remind us that God blesses us *before* we do any good works. It is important to receive the insights that call us to action as gifts. The actions we take are important as we find our way along the path of discipleship, but they do not make us righteous.

Individuals and groups need to establish a practice of prayer to support their theological reflection and their journeys as disciples. The following example illustrates the connection between insights gained in theological reflection and times of prayer.

> After four years as the rector of a large metropolitan Episcopal church, Brian found himself struggling with a sense of being swallowed up by the requirements of the institutional church. He felt as though he were caught in a web of demands that laced about him so tightly that he hardly had room to breathe. One evening he and a few others were reflecting on the story of Ruth and Boaz. Attention was drawn to how careful Boaz was to honor all the legal requirements that pertained to his relationship with Ruth. However, there was no sense that Boaz was constrained by these requirements; rather, he chose to use the norms of his community for the good of Ruth, even when this might have worked to his disadvantage.

> As the group was reflecting along these lines, Brian had a sense of being released from a great sense of constriction. "I realize that I have been tying myself in knots by wanting to control the results of everything I am involved in," he said with amazement. This insight was to have a marked effect on Brian's leadership of the parish, but he was not ready that evening to look at any practical implications. When the group

> closed with prayer Brian found himself deeply moved as
> someone gave thanks for the new freedom that Brian had
> found. "Yes, Lord," he said to himself, "Amen!"

New perspective may allow us to let go of behaviors and ideas
that have bound us. They may reveal behaviors destructive to
ourselves and to others and disclose a need for reconciliation
and forgiveness. Equally, new perspectives may heal and energize us, filling us with awe and gratitude for the gifts we have
received.

Whatever the contours of our insights, they are never for us
alone. Prayer and reflection move us beyond ourselves into compassionate action for others. We reflect and we pray so that we
can be open to the transformations that allow us to be more
faithfully agents of God's reign in the world.

Planning

Sometimes an insight produces a sudden change in behavior.

> Jane's daughter was two years old when she ran into her
> mother's lighted cigarette. Jane had been telling herself that
> her smoking was harmful only to herself. (After all, she had
> stopped while she was pregnant.) As she tended to the burn
> on her daughter's arm, the impact of the pain that she had
> caused was so strong that her dependence on tobacco van-
> ished; she has not smoked since.

In the example of Jane, insight and commitment to action
came simultaneously; no planning was needed. More often, however, insight does not lead automatically to action. Effective planning can prevent important insights from being lost in the rush
of a busy agenda and well-established habits.

Much has been written about how to plan effectively. One
simple method of planning to put an insight into practice is to
write down all the actions one might possibly take as a result of
the insight. Then examine each possible action by asking: Is the
action specific? Is it observable? Is it realistic? Amend the list of
actions, if necessary, after asking these questions. Then ask what,
if anything, you are in fact willing to do. Write that down, filling

in the details of where and when, being sure that there is a way to tell whether the planned action has been accomplished. For example:

> During a time of theological reflection with her Education for Ministry group, Sally gained some insight into an embattled relationship she had with a colleague at work. "I feel so threatened by her that I have a first-strike policy in place!" Sally understood how her own aggressive behavior might be escalating the hostility between them. As she began to plan what she might do differently, these were her first thoughts:
>
> • stop retaliating when she attacks me
> • apologize to her for attacking her
> • count to ten before I say anything to her
> • pray for the two of us
> • try to understand her point of view
>
> The group helped Sally to ask which of these actions was specific, observable, and realistic. After some discussion, Sally decided on the following plan for the next week:
>
> • Find two opportunities genuinely to agree with some point my colleague makes
> • Spend five minutes daily in prayer for the reconciliation of our relationship

The intent behind this method is to produce a workable plan for the next step to be taken. This step itself can then become the basis for further reflection. It is important to know when the step has been accomplished, so that there is accountability to the plan, and to maintain a sense that progress is being made. In this way even radical changes in behavior can be made one step at a time.

People

Companions are a great help as we explore the ways that open before us through our theological reflection. But it is here, right at the end of our reflective process, that we are most tempted to go it alone. Once we have been graced with insight and committed ourselves to some plan of action, we often mistakenly think that we need no further support. In the example above, Sally had learned that she was much more likely to follow through with a new and difficult course of action if she enlisted some support.

> Before the group closed for the evening, Sally asked Tom, a fellow participant, to help her be accountable to what she had chosen to do. They agreed that she would phone him in three days' time to let him know that she was spending the five minutes each day in prayer for reconciliation, and whether she had yet found an opportunity to agree with some point her colleague had made.

Our lives are full of demands from dozens of different sources. If we are to act on the insights that come from our theological reflection, we may need to increase our sense of accountability for the tentative plans we make. This is often the point where we need support to accomplish what is most important to us.

Processes for Personal Theological Reflection

Nine processes for theological reflection follow. All are developed from our basic framework for theological reflection: focusing on some aspect of experience; identifying the heart of the matter; putting the heart of the matter into conversation with the wisdom of the Christian heritage; and identifying new meaning and truths to take into daily living. Structurally many remain close to the movement toward insight. Each one begins with a different aspect of experience or source for theological reflection. All can be done alone or in a group setting. The symbols placed beside steps in the processes connect them back to the movement toward insight and the basic framework for theological reflection.

Beginning with a Life Situation

1. Narrate the situation or incident for reflection by writing it out or speaking it out loud. (Remember to remain close to the event and set aside current judgments about the situation. Use the "who, what, when, where, how" guidelines for entering experience.)

2. Listening to the narrative and attending to your physical sensations, identify the one or two central feelings that you experience most strongly in the situation. (Remember that these feelings capture the heart of the matter of the situation.)

3. Remain with those feelings in your body. Let them evoke images. List images until one comes that most captures the feelings. Use that image for the remainder of the reflection.

4. Sit with the image and explore it gently. Consider and question it in ways that open up new perspectives.
   - Listen for how God may be present and calling.
   - Consider what existence is like from within the image.
   - Notice what is broken and sorrowing in the image.
   - What possibilities for newness and for healing are present or implied?

   Write down the answers. Many enlightening thoughts may flow through your mind; note them briefly so you don't forget them.

5. Go back to the image and sit with it again. To what does the image take you in the Christian tradition? Brainstorm a list. Avoid asking why the image took

you there or trying to decide whether the piece of tradition "fits" with your original situation. If the image evokes something from the tradition, trust that a possible connection exists.

6. Pick one of the pieces of tradition that draws you. Explore that piece of tradition using the same questions that you used to explore the image. (If you want to explore more than one you can, but do not do more than two or your reflection will become too large and complex.)

7. Begin the conversation between the meanings in the image and in the tradition, using the two sets of answers to your questions.
   • What are the similarities?
   • What are the differences?
   • Is there a theme coming through both of them?
   • Is there a tension between them that is enlightening?

8. Organize the results of this conversation.
   • What emerges for you in this conversation?
   • What insights or questions does it raise for you?
   • Does anything out of this conversation shed light or provide a new angle of vision on your thoughts and actions and feelings in the original situation? On how you think or feel about it now?
   • Are you being called to some concrete action?
   • The next time you are in a similar situation, what do you want to remember or do differently?

9. How will you take the learnings of this reflection into your daily living? Write down your intention. Are you ready to take concrete steps to put this intention into practice? What specifically will you do? When will you begin? Who will support you?

Beginning with the Tradition I

This reflection can be done with any piece of the Christian heritage: a story of a saint, an event from church history, or a bishop's pastoral letter. The directions here presuppose a reading from Scripture out of the cycle of readings for Sundays in the year.

1. Read the Gospel passage for next Sunday. First read it to yourself slowly, then read it aloud slowly. Look at the language in the story, at the interchanges between and among people, at the shifts in action and energy.
   • What is this story about?
   • What is the heart of the matter?
   • Answer the question in terms of the text with its interactions and movements.

   As much as possible, set aside what you think you know about the particular piece of tradition and about Christianity generally. Attend to the text with fresh eyes. Let it be unfamiliar.

2. Sit with the Gospel passage until an image emerges that captures the central focal point in it.

3. Let the image lead you to your own situation in life.
   • What incidents from your experience does the image evoke for you? Pick one incident and explore it.
   • What were your thoughts and feelings in that situation?
   • What did you think about it until now?
   • What does the image tell you about that situation?
   • About your interpretation of it up to this point?
   • Is your interpretation confirmed, challenged, revised?

4. Move back from your exploration of your life experience to the original passage from Scripture.

- What do you see in the passage now that you did not see before?
- Has your attitude toward the passage or the characters in it changed?
- Do you hear its message differently now?

 5. What will you take with you from this reflection to your daily life?

Beginning with the Tradition II

This second example of theological reflection beginning from the tradition source starts with a story from Scripture and a meditation on the meaning of that story. Meditations and reflections in devotional books can also provide beginning points for theological reflection.

 1. Read the story of the woman bent over in Luke 13:10–17.

2. Read slowly the following meditation on the woman bent over:

A women bent over, "badly stooped—quite incapable of standing erect." No name, only an infirmity. We do not know how she has come to be bent over for eighteen years, whether from an illness or accident; whether from physical abuse or consuming work that destroys the body; whether from lack of adequate nutrition or a physical problem. A woman bent over, anonymous except for her deformity.

We do not know what brought the woman to the synagogue. We do not know if she came seeking cure or out of habit or out of some conscious awareness of her faith. We only know that she came. Twisted and hunched in her deformity, she came. Through the pain or the habit or the need, whatever brought her, the call to praise remains and she has hauled her twisted and stooped frame to the place of praise.

"When Jesus saw her he called her to him and said, 'woman you are free of your infirmity.' He laid his hand on her, and immediately she stood up straight and began thanking God." Luke does not tell us what she said or how she said it. He does not tell us whether she danced or cried, or sang, or snapped in two the staff she had used to haul herself around. He does not tell us what it was like for her to see straight ahead and around her instead of down. He does not tell us what went through her or through Jesus when they looked straight into each other's eyes, locked in a gaze acknowledging the power of a God who sustained them both.

The woman's transformation and praise are lost to us because in Luke's Gospel they serve to frame the conflict between the chief of the synagogue and Jesus. Luke presents the woman's healing and praise as an affront to the Sabbath in the mind of the synagogue chief. This allows Luke to direct our attention to Jesus' conversation with the synagogue chief, the conversation about whether a daughter of Abraham is worth as much as the ox or ass that any man takes out to water on the Sabbath.

The woman is a necessary bit player Luke uses for raising the stakes in the conflict between Jesus and the religious authorities of his day. So Luke tells us what the chief of the synagogue says in response to the woman's healing, but does not tell us what the woman says, only that she "began thanking God."

So, if we remain with Luke's agenda, we do not pause to notice the power of this woman. We do not notice the life that is flowing through her and out from her to all who hear her. We do not notice that she is an evangelist, sharing the good news of what God has done through Jesus. We miss her proclamation. We miss her praise.

How was this woman able to respond so unhesitatingly to God's healing power after eighteen years of pain and deformity? This question gives us an entrée into the story of this woman, a story that mainly is between the lines of the text. The text tells us three things: (1) the woman who was bent over for eighteen years was at the synagogue where Jesus was teaching; (2) when Jesus spoke to her and touched her she "stood up straight immediately"; and, (3) "she began thanking God." This minimal data, if we ponder it, reveals an amazing woman.

Chronic pain or illness becomes friendly after awhile, so familiar that they seep unknown into one's spirit and subtly and not so subtly possess one's standpoint and shapes one's perspective. The experience of chronic pain is terrifying, for it debilitates mind as well as body, destroying short and medium-term memory, disrupting relationships, sapping the desire to live. When people recover from chronic pain they often are disoriented. The pain had become so familiar that they are not sure who they are without it. If even a few months of chronic pain can shackle identity and limit freedom, what would eighteen years of pain and deformity do? And yet, we are confronted in Luke's story with a woman who unhesitatingly stood up straight. How was this possible?

In psychological language, the woman bent over shows us the ego strength and centered identity of a wise woman. She was able to experience what happened to her and all the feelings that went with it without letting them clog and clot her spirit. She did not identify herself with her deformity or her pain. She was able to experience pain, to let it move through her without letting it possess her. She was able to accept her situation without being determined by it. She had inner freedom in relation to her situation. Not a false sense of inner freedom that said that she was not touched by her deformity; she was, and she knew it. But a genuine inner freedom that is honest and accurate in assessing self and situations and is characterized by a gentle and compassionate self-acceptance.

So, when Jesus called the woman bent over she heard and responded. Why were her ears open to the people around her whom she could not see, stooped as she was? Why did she bother with the work around her at all, given the frequency of snide comments about people with infirmities deserving them because of sin? We know that she did bother and she did hear Jesus. When he said "Woman you are free of your infirmity," she stood up straight immediately. She did not hesitate. This wise woman was open to receiving God's gift of healing because she was open to her life, all of it, the parts she liked and the parts she did not like. The woman bent over knew how to move freely with grace.

How did she cultivate this ability, this woman whose deformity for eighteen years prevented her body ever from moving freely?

The answer, I suspect, is praise. Despite all the physical and social evidence to the contrary, this woman was in touch deeply within herself with the need to praise God. So she hauled herself to the synagogue for the service of public praise.

I am sure that the woman bent over recognized the irony of her situation, praising a God in the prayers of a tradition that also taught that those with infirmities were being punished for their sins. But this woman was in touch with her heritage at a deeper level than popular bias. She was connected to it through her own deep-seated sense of a need to praise God. Trusting that need, she acted on it and the ritual of praising, however foolish it may have looked to her neighbors, and at times to herself, kept the woman bent over cleansed and open and ready to receive God's healing when it came to her through Jesus.

3. Retrieve a time from your own experience when you or someone else was able to live fully and remain in tune with the depths of existence in the midst of suffering.
   - What was that experience like?
   - What thoughts and feelings were present in that situation?
   - How was reality different in that moment?
   - How did you or the other person relate to yourselves and the world?

4. Capture this way of being in an image or a sentence: "To live fully and deeply in the midst of suffering is [complete]. . . ."

5. What about human beings makes this kind of existence possible? Converse with the woman bent over about your image or sentence to answer this question.

6. How does our Christian tradition interpret this capacity in human beings?

7. How does our culture interpret this capacity in human beings?

8. What statement captures your position on this capacity in human beings?

9. What are you learning from this reflection that you will take with you to your life? What do you want the woman bent over to help you remember and do the next time you suffer?

Beginning with a Cultural Text I

Slogans, advertisements, novels, essays, great paintings, social institutions, social conflict, forests, these and much more from culture offer beginning points for reflection. This particular reflection begins with an essay, "The Space Crone." While the design is particular to this text, the same format can be used with any text.

For this particular reflection a clarification is in order on the word *crone.* The word is weighted with negative connotations in much of First World culture, conjuring up images of hags, undesirable, infertile old women. In the feminist movement, the term is being retrieved with its older connotations, those of a powerful woman whose fertility has moved beyond reproductive biology into a deep capacity to nurture all of life. The essay and this reflective process use the term in the second sense.

1. Read "The Space Crone" by Ursula Le Guin, p. 97.

2. Reflect on these questions:
   • What is the heart of the matter in this essay?
   • How do cultural and social structural elements of First World culture figure into the essay's central focus?

3. Who are the old women or crones in our Christian Scriptures and history? Brainstorm a list of them. Pick three and read their stories from Scripture or find their stories in sources from Christian history. Reflect on these questions:

- What is the central focus point in the situation of each of these women?
- How do cultural and social structural elements of their culture figure into their situations?

4. Think about your own experiences of old women/ crones throughout your life. Reflect on these questions:
    - As a child, what were your positions toward old women/crones?
    - What did you think about them?
    - How did these positions color the way you acted toward them?
    - What in the culture and social structure in which you grew up influenced your position toward crones?
    - What has been your experience of old women/ crones in the last two years?
    - How do you think about them now?
    - Articulate three positions of your own concerning old women/crones
    - What factors or elements in your current cultural and social structural contexts are influencing these positions?

5. What differences and similarities do you find among Le Guin's analysis of crones in First World culture, your positions on crones, and the positions toward crones in the material from tradition that you identified? How do these materials challenge one another? What confirmations do you see?

6. How does this material challenge you to change your behaviors and attitudes? How does it revise or confirm behaviors and attitudes you already hold?

7. What will you take away from this reflection?

The Space Crone[2]

The menopause is probably the least glamorous topic imaginable; and this is interesting, because it is one of the very few topics to which cling some shreds and remnants of taboo. A serious mention of menopause is usually met with uneasy silence; a sneering reference to it is usually met with relieved sniggers. Both the silence and the sniggering are pretty sure indications of taboo.

Most people would consider the old phrase "change of life" a euphemism for the medical term "menopause," but I, who am now going through the change, begin to wonder if it isn't the other way round. "Change of life" is too blunt a phrase, too factual. "Menopause," with its chime-suggestion of a mere pause after which things go on as before, is reassuringly trivial.

But the change is not trivial, and I wonder how many women are brave enough to carry it out wholeheartedly. They give up their reproductive capacity with more or less of a struggle, and when it's gone they think that's all there is to it. Well, at least I don't get the Curse any more, they say, and the only reason I felt so depressed sometimes was hormones. Now I'm myself again. But this is to evade the real challenge, and to lose, not only the capacity to ovulate, but the opportunity to become a Crone.

In the old days women who survived long enough to attain the menopause more often accepted the challenge. They had, after all, had practice. They had already changed their life radically once before, when they ceased to be virgins and became mature women/wives/matrons/mothers/mistresses/whores/etc. This change involved not only the physiological alterations of puberty—the shift from barren childhood to fruitful maturity—but a socially recognized alteration of being: a change of condition from the sacred to the profane.

With the secularization of virginity now complete, so that the once awesome term "virgin" is now a sneer or at best a slightly dated word for a person who hasn't copulated yet, the opportunity of gaining or regaining the dangerous/sacred condition of being at the Second Change has ceased to be apparent.

Virginity is now a mere preamble or waiting room to be got out of as soon as possible; it is without significance. Old age is similarly a waiting room, where you go after life's over and wait for cancer or a stroke. The years before and after the menstrual years are vestigial: the only meaningful condition left to women is that of fruitfulness. Curiously, this restriction of significance coincided with the development of chemicals and instruments that make fertility itself a meaningless or at least secondary characteristic of female maturity. The significance of maturity now is not the capacity to conceive but the mere ability to have sex. As this ability is shared by pubescent and by postclimacterics, the blurring of distinctions and elimination of opportunities is almost complete. There are no rites of passage because there is no significant change. The Triple Goddess has only one face: Marilyn Monroe's, maybe. The entire life of a woman from ten or twelve through seventy or eighty has become secular, uniform, changeless. As there is no longer any virtue in virginity, so there is no longer any meaning in menopause. It requires fanatical determination now to become a Crone.

Women have thus, by imitating the life condition of men, surrendered a very strong position of their own. Men are afraid of virgins, but they have a cure for their own fear and the virgin's virginity: fucking. Men are afraid of Crones, so afraid of them that their cure for virginity fails them; they know it won't work. Faced with the fulfilled Crone, all but the bravest men wilt and retreat, crestfallen and cockadroop.

Menopause Manor is not merely a defensive stronghold, however. It is a house or household, fully furnished with the necessities of life. In abandoning it, women have narrowed their domain and impoverished their souls. There are things the Old Woman can do, say, and think that the Woman cannot do, say, or think. The Woman has to give up more than her menstrual periods before she can do, say, or think them. She has got to change her life.

The nature of that change is now clearer than it used to be. Old age is not virginity but a third and new condition; the virgin must be celibate, but the Crone need not. There was a confusion there, which the separation of female sexuality from reproductive capacity, via modern contraceptives, has cleared up. Loss of fertility does not mean loss of desire and fulfillment. But it does

entail a change, a change involving matters even more important—if I may venture a heresy—than sex.

The woman who is willing to make that change must become
pregnant with herself, at last. She must bear herself, her third
self, her old age, with travail and alone. Not many will help her
with that birth. Certainly no male obstetrician will time her contractions, inject her with sedatives, stand ready with forceps, and
neatly stitch up the torn membranes. It's hard even to find an
old-fashioned midwife, these days. That pregnancy is long, that
labor is hard. Only one is harder, and that's the final one, the
one that men also must suffer and perform.

It may well be easier to die if you have already given birth to
others or yourself, at least once before. This would be an argument for going through all the discomfort and embarrassment
of becoming a Crone. Anyhow it seems a pity to have a built-in
rite of passage and to dodge it, evade it, and pretend nothing
has changed. That is to dodge and evade one's womanhood, to
pretend one's like a man. Men, once initiated, never get the second chance. They never change again. That's their loss, not ours.
Why borrow poverty?

Certainly the effort to remain unchanged, young, when the
body gives so impressive a signal of change as the menopause,
is gallant; but it is a stupid, self-sacrificial gallantry, better be-
fitting a boy of twenty than a woman of forty-five or fifty. Let
the athletes die young and laurel-crowned. Let the soldiers earn
the Purple Hearts. Let women die old, white-crowned, with human hearts.

If a space ship came by from the friendly natives of the fourth
planet of Altair, and the polite captain of the space ship said,
"We have room for one passenger; will you spare us a single
human being, so that we may converse at leisure during the long
trip back to Altair and learn from an exemplary person the
nature of the race?"—I suppose what most people would want
to do is provide them with a fine, bright, brave young man, highly
educated and in peak physical condition. A Russian cosmonaut
would be ideal (American astronauts are mostly too old). There
would surely be hundreds, thousands of volunteers, just such
young men, all worthy. But I would not pick any of them. Nor
would I pick any of the young women who would volunteer,

some out of magnanimity and intellectual courage, others out of a profound conviction that Altair couldn't possibly be any worse for a woman than Earth is.

What I would do is go down to the local Woolworth's, or the local village marketplace, and pick an old woman, over sixty, from behind the costume jewelry counter or the betel-nut booth. Her hair would not be red or blonde or lustrous dark, her skin would not be dewy fresh, she would not have the secret of eternal youth. She might, however, show you a small snapshot of her grandson, who is working in Nairobi. She is a bit vague about where Nairobi is, but extremely proud of the grandson. She has worked hard at small, unimportant jobs all her life, jobs like cooking, cleaning, bringing up kids, selling little objects of adornment or pleasure to other people. She was a virgin once, a long time ago, and then a sexually potent fertile female, and then went through menopause. She has given birth several times and faced death several times—the same times. She is facing the final birth/death a little more nearly and clearly everyday now. Sometimes her feet hurt something terrible. She never was educated to anything like her capacity, and that is a shameful waste and cannot be hidden from Altair. And anyhow she's not dumb. She has a stock of sense, wit, patience, and experiential shrewdness, which the Altairians might, or might not, perceive as wisdom. If they are wiser than we, then of course we don't know how they'd perceive it. But if they are wiser than we, they may know how to perceive that inmost mind and heart which we, working on mere guess and hope, proclaim to be humane. In any case, since they are curious and kindly, let's give them the best we have to give.

The trouble is, she will be very reluctant to volunteer. "What would an old woman like me do on Altair?" she'll say. "You ought to send one of those scientist men, they can talk to those funny-looking green people. Maybe Dr. Kissinger should go. What about sending the Shaman?" It will be very hard to explain to her that we want her to go because only a person who has experienced, accepted, and acted the entire human condition—the essential quality of which is Change—can fairly represent humanity. "Me?" she'll say, just a trifle slyly. "But I never did anything."

But it won't wash. She knows, though she won't admit it, that Dr. Kissinger has not gone and will never go where she has gone, that the scientist and the shamans have not done what she has done. Into the space ship, Granny.

Beginning with Cultural Text II

The flow of reflections, beginning with cultural texts, is from the *cultural situation* to the *tradition* and our own *experience.* Whether we begin with a written cultural text or a cultural text in some other medium, such as art or technology, we build our reflection out of the material from these three sources.

A fresh way to begin theological reflection is to gather a variety of cultural texts dealing with a particular issue or problem, the question of aging or the plight of ancient forests or the plight of inner cities, for example. The following reflection focuses on aging.

1. Find examples of the way old men and women from First World culture are represented in print media, films, on broadcast news, in books.

2. Think about the examples you have collected in light of the following questions:
   - How are old men and women portrayed in your examples?
   - Is the presentation dominantly negative, positive, a mix of the two? Is the presentation different by gender?
   - How do dominant cultural values and biases influence the presentation of old women and men in your examples?
   - What social structural elements, for example, work, consumption, family patterns, influence the presentation and situation of old people?

3. Who are the old women and men in our Christian Scriptures and history? Brainstorm a list of them.

Pick three and read their stories from Scripture or find their stories in sources from Christian history. Reflect on these questions:

- What is the central point in the situation of each of these women or men?
- How do cultural and social structural elements of their culture figure into their situations?

4. Think about your own experiences of old men and women throughout your life. Reflect on these questions:

- As a child, what were your positions toward old people?
- What did you think about them?
- How did these positions color the way you acted toward them?
- What in the culture and social structure in which you grew up influenced your position toward old people?
- What has been your experience of old women and men in the last two years?
- How do you think about them now?
- Articulate three positions of your own concerning old women and men.
- What factors or elements in your current cultural and social structural contexts are influencing these positions?

5. What differences and similarities do you find among the presentation of old men and women in your examples from First World culture, your positions on old people, and the positions toward old men and women in the material from tradition that you identified? How do these materials challenge one another? What confirmations do you see?

6. How does this material challenge you to change your behaviors and attitudes? How does it revise or confirm behaviors and attitudes you already hold?

7. What will you take away from this reflection?

Beginning with a Theme

Sometimes a theme will emerge in our lives and invite reflection. Certain seasons of the liturgical year, major life transitions, and other events may focus our attention on a particular theme such as birth, rebirth, grief, creativity, relationship. Such themes can provide a focus for theological reflection. This particular design is built around the theme of brokenness.

 1. Take a paper cup and bend it in half. Set the cup in front of you and sit quietly looking at it. Describe the bent cup.
- How is it broken?
- What can or can't be done with it?
- How is a bent cup usually regarded?
- What happens to bent cups?

 2. Close your eyes and breathe deeply. Moving through your own life experience, find times when you were a "bent cup." Briefly note one from your childhood, one from your young adulthood, one from the past year. Explore each of these situations.
- What were your key thoughts and feelings?
- How were you broken?
- What did you find yourself able and unable to do?
- How do you think others regarded you and treated you?
- What happened in each situation?

Write a paragraph that begins: "When I am a bent cup I . . ."

 3. Go back to the image—bent cup—and let it lead you into the Christian tradition. What situations, people, passages, from Scripture and Christian history are captured by the image? Brainstorm. Pick one and explore it.
- What thoughts and feelings are in the passage?
- What is the brokenness?

- What are people able and unable to do in the story?
- How are the broken ones treated?
- What happens in the situation?

Write a paragraph which begins: "In Scripture/ Christian history a bent cup . . ."

4. Compare and contrast the experience of and perspectives on being a bent cup from your own lived narrative, the Christian heritage, and common attitudes toward brokenness in our culture. From this comparison and contrast, what do you now believe about being a bent cup? Write a statement about bent-cup experiences that you are willing to claim as your own.

5. What do you want to remember or do differently the next time you find yourself in the position or situation of a bent cup?

Beginning with Personal Positions

Positions are those convictions that we are willing to defend. Part of the journey in faith involves noticing what our positions are, especially our theological positions, thinking about their sources, and assessing them in light of our best understanding of our religious heritage, our lived narrative, and wisdom from our culture. This reflection process begins this exploration with positions on the church. It can be used to reflect theologically on positions involving any theological theme.

1. List ten statements that you hold about the church. (Remember that positions are convictions for which you are willing to argue.)

2. Pick the three statements most important to you and explore their origins.
   - From where did your position come?

- What in your lived narrative contributed to them?
- What from your cultural context contributed to them?
- What from the Christian heritage contributed to them?

3. Why are these positions important to you? Answer this question by writing a series of statements beginning, "I believe . . . about the church because . . ." For each statement, repeat the process completing the sentence, "I believe . . . because . . ."
   - What do your answers tell you about your vision of the church?
   - What is the core understanding or essence of the church in your positions?

4. What in Christian tradition confirms the central core of the church as you have described it? Brainstorm a list. What in Christian tradition challenges the vision of the church as you have described it? Brainstorm a list.

5. Explore one or two items from each list. Can you find any commonality in them? Can you articulate the tension or attraction between them?

6. How does your exploration lead you to reconsider your vision of the crucial center of the church?
   - What in your original positions are you still willing to defend?
   - Are they confirmed? How?
   - Do you need to revise them? How?
   - Can the positions be more accurately stated?
   - Are they really grounded in the Christian heritage? Where?
   - Are your positions equally, more, or less important than the core or essence of the church for you that you identified from them? Why? Why not?

7. Restate your positions from a vision/viewpoint of the central core of the church as you identified it. How will your experience of and participation in the church differ, if you relate to the church out of these statements rather than the previous ones?

 8. What will you take away with you to your daily living from this reflection?

Beginning with Religious Experiences

Religious experiences are part of our lives. Encounters with nature, great art or music, people, books, personal struggle and many more interactions evoke religious experiences. These encounters lead us to an awareness of the transcendent impinging on our lives. Religious experiences also can be starting points for theological reflection.

 1. Briefly jot down experiences of the transcendent in your life, times during which you experienced God's touch or an intensity of a reality that transcends our ordinary, taken-for-granted world. Pick an experience from your youth, young adulthood, the past ten years, the past five years, the past two months. (The time intervals you use will vary depending on your age. If you are young, use shorter periods. If you are midlife or older, use ten- or twenty-year periods until the past two years.) Take each experience in turn.

 2. Narrate the situation briefly. Identify the key feeling it contains and an image that captures it.

 3. Going back to each image, answer in turn the following questions for reflection:
   • What does that image reveal about how God is at work in the world?

- What counts as God's work in the world in this image?
- What does the image reveal about how God actually relates to people?
- Why is this important?

4. Review your answers to the questions. What is the range of answers? What are the commonalities?

5. Define a position of your own about how God works in the world. Are you willing to defend this statement? If so, why? If not, why not?

6. What will you take away to your search for God in your daily life from this reflection?

Reading Another's Theological Text

Books and articles in theology, spirituality, and ministry also provide starting points for theological reflection. When we begin with another's theological text our process tends primarily to address the positions of the author in relation to our own positions.

We engage in this process by reading another's text as a dialogue partner. To do so we must come to understand the content, perspective, and approach of the text. Then we can look jointly with it at the particular projects, concerns, problems, or issues that led us to read the text. This is a two-step process involving both the critical reading of a theological text and a creative conversation with it.

Critical Reading of a Theological Text

The critical reading of a theological text involves two broad concepts: *coherence* and *adequacy*. Coherence has to do with the argument of the text; does it hold together? Does the writer do what she says she will do? Does what he says make sense? Would what she says be understandable to a nonbeliever, willing for the sake of discussion to acknowledge the author's presuppositions? Another word for coherence in this context is intelligibility.

Adequacy refers to how well the author has expressed her position in light of Scripture, the theological heritage, contemporary humanistic and social-scientific scholarship, and the faith experience of the contemporary Christian community. Another way to talk about adequacy is to ask: Has the author expressed the faith with integrity? Integrity here involves more than literal content. It also involves tone and style. Does the author convey the depth and quality of the faith experience of Christians?

The following questions guide a critical reading of a theological text:

1. What does the author say? Summarize the main points in your own words.

2. What is her concern or the religious issue that she addresses? Is the stated issue or concern the only one or is there another unstated, and perhaps more important, one?

3. Against what or whom does the author seem to be arguing?

4. What does the author say he will do in the text? What does she actually do?

5. What are the author's presuppositions, basic images, hidden agenda?

6. What are the author's sources? Tradition, action, culture, positions? Does the author use some more than others? Give more authority to one than another?

7. What is the author's method? How does she actually proceed in the text? How does he identify data from the sources, correlate that data, and identify new insights?

8. Is what the author says adequate? Does it fit with the best understanding of the tradition and cultural knowledge?

Creative Conversation with a Theological Text

We do a critical reading of a theological text as part of our effort to understand what the author is saying so that we can converse creatively with the author about topics or projects. The aim here is real conversation, with the reciprocal listening, challenging, and clarification that characterize good conversation between persons. Such conversation can occur only after we have come to understand and to respect our conversation partner, in this case the text. The question for creative conversation is: What insights, applications, or approaches does this text have that are applicable to my own projects? These insights and applications might be positive and they might be negative. However the conversation is structured, it needs to involve conversation between oneself and the text about something. This triadic structure is an essential part of conversation and understanding.

Questions that will guide a creative conversation with a theological text are:

1. How is the text's statement and approach to the project, concern, or issue similar to and different from my own?
   - Does it confirm my idea and my approach to it?
   - Does it challenge me to refine or revise my idea and my approach to it?

2. What insights or application does the text have for my project?
   - What ideas might I want to adopt and convey to others?
   - What images or phrases capture a vision that I want to transmit?
   - What attitudes or perspectives in the text might I want to adopt as my own and bring to others?
   - What approaches to a question or problem that work for the author's situation might I want to adopt or translate for my situation?

Summary

Honesty, time, practice, prayer, study, and support help us to make theological reflection part of our journeys in faith. We take on the discipline because we know the call to the journey into intensification, into living our lives fully, all aspects of them. We make theological reflection part of our practice when we respond to the call to transformation, to religious maturity. Theological reflection forms us and shapes us. It deepens our discipleship, strengthens our commitment, and at the same time leaves us increasingly open to life.

5

~

Guiding Groups in
Theological Reflection

Theological Reflection
as a Ministerial Resource

Theological reflection changes lives. The practice of theological reflection helps us take religious insights, which are fleeting, and gradually move them into our permanent structures of perceiving and interpreting experience. It invites us to pause to reinterpret past experiences more adequately in light of our faith so that our daily lives can be lived more faithfully. Theological reflection slows us down, gets us beyond our chronic human embarrassment and anxiety, and creates a climate for grace to transform us. When theological reflection works it helps us to act a little differently. It unblocks our spirit by disciplining and refining our habitual processes for making meaning of our experience.

All this makes theological reflection a powerful resource for ministers. It allows us to let the grace present in our ministerial experience fund and energize us. It helps us become more discerning and perceptive in our ministerial interactions. It increases our appreciation of how our ministry continues the deeds of the kingdom begun by Jesus. Theological reflection deepens the practice of ministry and nurtures ministers' souls. This is true whether our ministry takes place in the workplace, the parish, or our local community.

Ministers in leadership positions have a special responsibility to learn about and use theological reflection. Whether we head a professional staff, organize and support volunteers, or companion people in business, agriculture, government, education, human services, and the arts on their spiritual journeys, we must help those with whom we work develop the practice of theological reflection. Assisting them to bring their life experience into dynamic conversation with the wisdom of the Christian heritage creates contexts for long-lasting insight and significant growth in faith.

Preliminaries to Leading Others in Theological Reflection

Theological Reflection: A Call to Religious Maturity

The call to lead others into theological reflection should not be taken lightly. When we invite people into theological reflection as part of their journeys in faith we invite them to recast their relationship with their religious heritage. We must be clear about our own motivation and commitment for asking people to begin this journey. Using theological reflection to persuade people to adopt our own particular theological, ecclesial, or political positions twists and abuses the power of our theological heritage. Throughout Christianity's history, such manipulations of the heritage have caused only negative consequences, both for people and for the tradition.

Theological knowledge, like all truth and wisdom, is both liberating and dangerous. The mentor in theological reflection, like guides on all journeys, can lead others to sin or grace or both. If we invite people on the journey we must be willing to spend time with them while they learn the art of theological reflection and begin to discern grace-filled from sinful opportunities in their lives.

When adults respond to the opportunity for theological reflection, they often do so with mixed motivations. Some come believing that theology is a set of general rules to be learned and applied. They come in order to learn the rules and how to apply them to improve their lives. These adults approach the tradition developmentally from a psychic and social standpoint in which they assume that there is a single authority, one outside of themselves, which is always correct and always ready with answers to their questions.

These adults tend to think of religion as the repetition of eternally true statements. They do not understand that faith statements, while vital in their original context, are diminished or twisted when divorced from their original context, and repeated without being newly made our own. They do not realize that such regurgitated theology serves only to reinforce arrangements of power, values, and resources that privilege a few and impoverish many. Adults who approach theological reflection from this perspective often experience the tradition imposing impossible standards and overwhelming moralistic obligations. They do not hear the vital challenge the tradition contains.

Others come to theological reflection eager to learn what the tradition teaches and more than eager to give their views to anyone who will listen. Often these adults are quite unwilling to pay attention to their own experience, especially its affective dimensions. They want theological knowledge for security, or status, or power. They are unaware of the deep fear inside of them that they might encounter God in their experience.

Still others come to theological reflection ready to bend and mold the Christian heritage into support for their particular agenda. They often are filled with righteous indignation at the church, society, and themselves for not living as Christians should. The anxiety and urgency that consume them block their capacity to reflect.

It can be a daunting task to lead a group with these mixed expectations and motivations into theological reflection. Often members are so preoccupied with performing the process correctly and achieving the "right" outcome that genuine reflection is short-circuited. They can become very uncomfortable also when they discover that the Christian tradition does not automatically reinforce their dearly held positions about God, women's roles in society, work, or anything else. They may be deeply disturbed by the dawning realization that there is no single appropriate Christian answer to all situations.

Still ministers must not shirk the call to invite others into theological conversation. By guiding people in theological reflection ministers provide them the opportunity to relate to their religious heritage from a more mature psychic and social standpoint. Religiously mature people know their thoughts, feelings, and desires and can articulate them. They notice and care about their own and others' lives and inner processes. They understand that truth has contexts, that knower and known are intimately connected. Adults in this standpoint are capable of entering into genuine conversation about things that matter to them. Religiously mature people speak compassionately and intelligently from a centered, relational self.

Maturity brings an altered relationship with one's religious heritage. The tradition becomes known as the collective wisdom of the past and present community. The tradition carries particular weight as trustworthy, but it is not the single absolute in someone's life. There are no single absolutes. The tradition becomes a rich mixture of wisdom that people befriend. As with most good conversation partners, the tradition begins to provide both delightful and discomfiting surprises, opening new angles of vision on our lives. At this stage adults have befriended the Christian heritage.

Through the practice of theological reflection with groups, ministers can help adults to understand that the tradition is dynamic and growing. They can help people come to see that the tradition is larger than any individual's or group's view of it. Ministers can help adults begin to understand that they themselves transmit and shape the tradition, just as it has borne, formed, and continues to form them. Through theological reflection adults come to grasp the extent to which the tradition is both stable and fluid. They begin to know cognitively and affectively that faithfulness demands reinterpretation of the tradition for new settings. Faithfulness demands a relationship to our tradition in which it can criticize circumstances, attitudes, and actions that run counter to the gospel. Our relationship to our tradition is a process of mutual sustenance and transformation.

Contextual Factors in Calling Adults
to Theological Reflection

When inviting adults on the journey into theological reflection a facilitator must be cognizant of the human commitments required. The previous chapter identified the most basic ones as honesty, time, and grounding in study, prayer, and people skills. Facilitators of theological reflection need to make an accurate and candid assessment of them in relation to self and those for whom we will be facilitating theological reflection.

If our comments about honesty, vulnerability, and courage as prerequisites for theological reflection are accurate, then a facilitator of theological reflection must honor these qualities in the persons with whom she works. He must respect the integrity to which the process of theological reflection calls adults. Moreover, the facilitator can help a group recognize and honor the qualities of honesty and courage in one another. So, honoring the integrity of the people in a group contributes significantly to creating a context where real conversation can occur and insights arise.

In chapter 4 we noted that learning theological reflection takes time. An artful practice cannot be learned and refined overnight. Ministers, keenly aware of urgent needs and heavy responsibilities, can easily succumb to the cultural temptation to demand quick solutions and fast changes in seeking programs that offer significant impact but require little participant investment. This is nonsense. Those who are called by Christian communities to be guides and companions on our journeys in faith must be willing to take the time required to help us appropriate the art of theological reflection. The People of God do not need ministers who engage in a "let's pretend" or a "spiritual hit-and-run artist" ministry. There is something seriously amiss when pastors, staffs, and members of Christian congregations prefer the busyness of projects and programs to the power of the encounter with God in serious theological reflection.

The designated facilitator for a theological reflection group bears particular responsibility for helping that group develop the study, prayer, and interpersonal skills that contribute to quality theological reflection. Because theological reflection withers unless a group is deepening its knowledge and appropriation of its Christian heritage, the facilitator must first encourage study and be studying herself. Second, the facilitator can both model leading communal prayer and then support group members, providing a foundation and energy-source of theological reflection for the group. Third, and most especially, the facilitator is responsible for helping the group establish and then live by norms that reflect effective human interaction skills: listening, clarifying, saying "I," engaging in conflict appropriately, sensitively supporting one another, and more.

In terms of study, prayer, and people skills, the facilitator needs to be guided by his primary intention for the group: creating a context where genuine conversation between the people's experience and the Christian heritage can happen so that faithful, life-giving insights may emerge. This intention becomes a criterion for evaluating appropriate types of intervention necessary for leading a group in theological reflection. It also helps the facilitator to discriminate between a theological reflection group and other kinds of groups. For instance, while a theological reflection group differs from a human-relations-skills training group, its primary task, theological reflection, does require that participants develop basic communication skills. Similarly, while a theological reflection group is not a therapy group, though its secondary result often is healing, attention to the needs of participants and awareness of their developmental stages is helpful to a facilitator.

Guidelines for Using Theological Reflection

When considering the task of leading others in theological reflection we need to think through the specifics of doing it with a particular group in a given setting. The most important considerations fall under "the five P's": people, purpose, parameters, presence, and process.

People

People do theological reflection. If we want to lead a group in this activity we need to think about the people and identify what and how much we know about them. What are their conceptual and interpersonal skills? Are they comfortable with abstract and imaginative thinking? Are they reticent to speak or do they share openly? What is their familiarity with the Christian tradition? Is this a group that is ongoing or will it exist only for two or three sessions? Is this a group of people who are gathered around a task that theological reflection will enhance or are they coming specifically for theological reflection and faith development? Are these adults whose relationships outside of this setting may impinge on how openly they feel they can share within it? What are the ages of the participants in this group? What are their socioeconomic and cultural backgrounds? What are their longings and desires? What are their hurts and joys? Thinking about these questions helps us develop a more accurate and nuanced understanding of the people with whom we will do theological reflection.

Purpose

We undertake theological reflection with a purpose in mind. We need to think about the purpose for theological reflection in terms of each session and in terms of the overall set of sessions. Why are we facilitating theological reflection with these people? Is it a baptismal preparation series for parents in which we want to link sacramental theology with their lived experience? Is it a group of older women who meet for lunch after Mass once a week and who want to "do something more"? Perhaps our purpose with them is to break open the meaning of their experiences in light of women of faith in our Christian heritage. Is it a group of managers who want to relate their faith to their work world? Is it families we meet on chaplaincy rounds? Is it abused women at a shelter? Is it a group of lectors in the parish who read well but who do not seem to understand fully what reading for a community in the context of liturgy is about?

Articulating the purpose for theological reflection clearly and simply is vital and often difficult. Yet clarity about our purpose in leading others in theological reflection helps us develop or select an appropriate reflective design and serves as a plumb stone when leading people through a process. In any theological reflection our goal is to create a reflective context within which the people can relate some part of their experience to the wisdom of the Christian heritage.

Parameters

Parameters are the elastic boundaries of or limits on theological reflection for a particular group. Are the members known to one another or are they strangers? Is it a large or small group? What are the factors in the people's lives outside of this setting that impinge on it? The answers to such questions suggest much about what kinds of reflective designs are appropriate. In what physical setting will we meet? Can newsprint, clay, or music be used in it? Is it a private environment where confidential sharing can occur? Is it an impersonal, large space? How much time is there for the session? How much of that time will be required for other activities according to the customs of these adults or this particular group? Has this group come with a particular request for assistance around a particular topic? Is the initiative in introducing theological reflection ours? Is this group compulsory or voluntary?

Presence

Theological reflection requires a facilitator's energy and focused presence to the group. If we are working with a very large group we can give them worksheets or have them work with partners or write in journals, or in other ways lead them through a reflective process without having to be intimately present to each one. Such a distanced presence is quite different from the intimate setting of working with a smaller group of six to ten people. Then the quality of our personal presence as the facilitator becomes much more important to the process. To lead a small group skillfully in theological reflection we need to have some genuine care and compassion for these people. Can we invite others to reflect on life experiences and to share their reflections and questions unless we are willing to do the same?

As a facilitator or leader of theological reflection, it is very important for us to be honest with ourselves about our attitude toward and investment in the people with whom we are working. How do they and theological reflection fit into our own life journey and ministerial tasks? How much of ourselves are we willing to give this group? Do we like these people or dislike them? How capable are we of listening openly and responding appropriately to their questions, conflicts, struggles, and joys?

Process

Once we have considered people, purpose, parameters, and presence, we are ready to select or develop a particular *process* or design to use for theological reflection. The design should be appropriate to the people with whom we will work and to the constraints of our setting, group size, time limits, and such. Any effective design will contain the elements in the basic framework for theological reflection: (1) focusing on some aspect of experience; (2) describing that experience to identify the heart of the matter; (3) putting the heart of the matter into conversation with the wisdom of the Christian heritage; (4) identifying new meanings and truths to take back to daily living. The designs included in chapter 4 illustrate the variety of ways that theological reflection processes can be structured. The question to ask in assessing these designs or others is: Can this design accomplish my purpose for theological reflection with this group?

The basic framework for theological reflection can also assist in developing new designs for theological reflection around particular purposes with particular groups. Once we are clear about our purpose, we can think through the developmental process using the steps of the framework. The next chapter focuses on using the framework to develop designs for theological reflection.

Remember the Larger Context

Whatever design we use for theological reflection with a group, we need to draw on our resources of group facilitation and leadership skills. Theological reflection is a process and moves most freely in a group that has learned how to work together, to speak clearly together, to support and challenge one another.

We want to remember that theological reflection is a discipline of a community of faith. This means that prayer should be part of the context for theological reflection in the life of a group. Prayer grounds a group in its Christian heritage.

There is no way to predict or predetermine the outcome of a theological reflection process. Nor should the facilitator try to do so. Facilitators intend to be attuned to the key feelings, images, themes, and questions that arise when guiding a reflective process. They work to create a context where silence is permissible and where all who choose to speak have a chance to do so. Facilitators want to support people to listen carefully. If challenge occurs among members of the group over particular ideas or interpretations, facilitators intervene to promote effective and respectful conflict. Facilitators also encourage authentic expressions of celebration and gratitude in a group.

Facilitating theological reflection is an artful practice. We may have a fine design for reflection, but the design is not actual theological reflection, any more than an artist's vision is the picture or sculpture she produces. A facilitator's primary task in theological reflection is actually to guide a group through reflection. An artful facilitator uses a particular design and the basic framework for theological reflection as resources but nudges the group so that neither her design nor other agenda of the group blocks the actual reflective process.

This means that the facilitator is willing to live in some tension as he guides the group and is willing to help the group notice what they are doing and learn when it is or is not theological reflection. Chattering or grousing, while possibly valuable for the group's maintenance, are not theological reflection and should not be confused with it. Analyzing a situation psychologically is not theological reflection. Problem-solving together is not theological reflection. The issue here is not that any other activity is wrong or bad, but that it simply is not theological reflection.

Neither is a group doing theological reflection when it uses a reflective design that is rigid and boring and predictable, so that participants know what the outcome will be within a few minutes of beginning the process. When a particular design, instead of the reflective process, becomes the focus of attention, then theological reflection has been short-circuited.

The artful facilitator of theological reflection trusts that the group's reflective process is valuable, that it is a container for faith-filled, life-giving insight. In this sense the facilitator is the midwife of the movement toward insight.

Summary

Ministers have a choice. They can ignore or embrace theological reflection as a resource for their own development and for the growth in faith of those with whom they work. Theological reflection offers a powerful strategy for forming religiously mature, adult Christians.

The choice to use theological reflection, however, demands that a minister accept the vocation to leadership in the spiritual formation of individuals and communities. It requires ministers to make decisions about personal investment and time that put the cultivation of wisdom at the top of their goals.

The five P's—people, purpose, parameters, presence, process—are tools for taking the first step in using theological reflection. That step should not be taken, however, until ministers have considered and accepted the responsibilities that facilitating theological reflection entails.

6

Creating Designs for Theological Reflection

Understanding the basic framework for theological reflection helps us to facilitate it effectively. Learning to use the framework as a resource for developing creative designs for theological reflection is equally important. This chapter presents options and possibilities for designing theological reflection based on each section of the basic framework.

Focusing on Experience or How to Identify and Select Material from Sources

Undifferentiated experience is too encompassing to be the subject for fruitful reflection, so theologians divide experience into aspects, commonly known as sources. Sources provide the relevant data that we want to incorporate into our theological reflection. In chapter 3 we presented the following sources: action (lived narrative), tradition (Scripture, church history, theology, popular lore), culture (culture, social structure, physical environment), and positions (convictions for which one is willing to argue).

Thinking about experience in terms of its aspects or sources constitutes the first phase in developing processes for theological reflection. Once we are clear on the purpose, we must address three questions in order to design a process for theological reflection:

(1) Given our purpose, will we use the action, culture, tradition, and/or position sources? We need to draw on at least two of them and one must be tradition for our reflection to be theological.
(2) How will we have the group select and hone in on material from each source?
(3) With which source will we begin the reflective process?

A design for theological reflection can begin by attending to data from any one of the sources. The purpose for the theological reflection and the parameters and people considerations often suggest the appropriate place to begin.

At this point in creating a design the questions we shape to direct people's attention to experience are important. These questions determine how and where a group directs its attention. For example, we can access the action source with the following instructions:

(1) Reflecting on your life this past month, what incident invites your further reflection?
(2) Identify times in your experience when you felt able to live freely.

Notice that the first instruction guides a group to the action source in an open-ended way. The facilitator will not know what a presenter in the group will share. Hence, the facilitator will need a process that can work flexibly with a variety of incidents from the action source. The second instruction guides a group to the action source in a way that orients them to a particular kind of experience, namely, one of having been able to love freely. This question suggests a design built around a theme.

The shape of questions for directing a group's attention to some elements of experience will vary depending on the source with which the reflection starts. Here are some examples:

Action Source:
• Answer question X, for example, what is important to you about family?, with a narrative.
• What incident from your life invites reflection?

• Find an incident in your life when you felt powerless to do what you wanted to do.

Culture Source:
• What are five commonly held beliefs about the role of a mother in our culture?
• How does our economic system contribute to homelessness and hunger?
• How has this locale changed during the past five years?
• Is the water that comes from your kitchen faucet fit to drink?

Tradition Source:
• What is the Gospel story from last Sunday about?
• In what Gospel story do you find Jesus' words or actions most perplexing?
• In what incidents from the history of Christianity were religious institutions faithful to the gospel?

Position Source:
• What are three statements about Christianity for which you would argue?
• What is the Christian belief most central to your faith?
• How is the Bible the Word of God?
• What is your definition of human nature?

Notice that these questions focus a group on a limited amount of material from one of the sources. A group cannot engage in effective theological reflection if it tries to use too much material from any one source. While any one of these questions can provide a starting point for a theological reflection, which one a facilitator chooses will direct a reflection in a particular direction.

Identifying the Heart of the Matter or Determining the Crux of Our Reflection

Once we have decided what sources to use, how to have people identify and select data from them, and with which source to begin the reflection, the next step is to decide how the individuals or the group will identify the heart of the matter. What is the central issue or tension or theme in the material to which they have turned their attention? Can a feeling or image capture it? Might a sentence statement that expresses the tension work more effectively? If this reflection is organized around a chosen theme, how should that theme be expressed as the focal point of the reflection?

Determining the core of an experience for reflection is not easy. We bring experiences to reflection when we do not fully understand their meaning. This is true whether we bring a piece of our lived narrative, something from tradition, material from our culture, or our position on an issue for reflection. Almost always the experience we bring for reflection is complex. It may contain more than one focal point from which valuable reflection could begin.

There is no single way to articulate the heart of the matter of an experience. The statement may be in the form of a feeling or image such as we use in the movement toward insight. It may be a sentence that captures the tension in a situation: "I want to think that I have earned the comforts of a middle-class life but I am disturbed when I meet homeless and hungry people who share my background and education." It may be a detailed analysis of what happens to the water that runs through our kitchen faucet from its source to our glass. It may be a passage from Scripture that disturbs us in its presentation of discipleship, for example, "Let the dead bury their own dead" (Luke 9:60).

While there is no single way to articulate the heart of the matter, there are guidelines that will help state it in a way that contributes to a richer reflective process. The statement of the crux of an experience brought for reflection should capture some of the emotional energy of that experience. We reflect on experiences that our habitual meaning-making processes cannot interpret adequately. The way we know that such experiences do not fit into our current interpretive framework is that they remain with us. They haunt our thoughts, enrich our daydreams, relax or tense our muscles. The statement of the heart of the matter should capture some of this emotional energy.

For example, if I bring for reflection an experience of inner conflict concerning my relative economic affluence and the poverty of the people I step over on my way to the office each day, I might put the heart of the matter this way: "I want to believe that I have earned my position and comfort, *but* I know that these unemployed street people are as well-educated and bright as I am." Such a statement captures the inner tension of the situation, the conflict between a position that I want to hold and the social and economic realities of my culture. Or I might bring for reflection Jesus' words in Luke's Gospel, "Let the dead bury their own dead." Then my statement of the heart of the matter might be: "This saying of Jesus, so contradictory to Jesus' culture and to my own desires to respect the needs of my family members, conveys an unbounded quality to true discipleship that is frightening." This statement of the crux of the passage brought for reflection includes the affective energy involved in encountering the passage.

While we want the statement of the heart of the matter to retain the affective energy from our experience, we also want it to remove us slightly from the intensity and immediacy of those feelings. Articulating the focal point of a narrated experience in a feeling or image, as we do in the movement toward insight, provides both the affective connection and the slightly different relationship to the experience. This slightly altered relationship to the event allows for new perspectives on it. Similarly, we can use an issue statement, formulated in terms of the tension between two divergent pulls—"I want *but* I want"—to state the central focus of an experience for reflection. Shaping such a statement helps provide the altered relationship to the experience that we need in order to be able to reflect. It does so, however, without so cutting us off from the original experience that our reflection has no impact.

The statement of the focal point of an experience must be limited. If the epicenter of the reflection is too broad the reflection will be too diffuse and generalized for significant insights to occur. It makes moving through a reflection process difficult. It requires us to spend so much time trying to keep track of the entire incident that we cannot reflect in any depth.

When stating the core of reflection we must beware of presenting a position in disguise. Our habitual meaning-making processes move naturally in the direction of fitting events into our present interpretive framework. Our positions are supported by and reinforce that interpretive framework. So it is easy for a position statement to slip in disguised as a statement of the heart of the matter for reflection. For example, if I share for reflection an event in which I received an unexpected award for my professional competence and then was overcome with a sense of unworthiness, I might be drawn quickly to focus the reflection on my fear of success. Holding the position that I have a problem with success would lead me to do so. Perhaps, in this event, the more revelatory potential rests in the meaning of receiving a surprising gift.

Stating the heart of the matter of an experience for reflection requires practice. It requires listening to the experience brought for reflection with open minds and perceptive hearts. A facilitator's temptation is to think that he or she understands the significant issue in the experience too quickly. Work to help the group state it. Keep these guidelines in mind:

(1) The statement should contain the affective energy of the experiences.
(2) The statement should provide a slightly altered relationship to the original experience in order to provide new perspectives on it.
(3) The statement needs a narrow enough focus to be manageable for reflection.
(4) The statement should be as free as possible of hidden position statements.

These guidelines hold regardless of which source provides the starting point for a reflection.

Creating a Conversation or Correlating Material from the Sources

Defining Correlation

Correlation names the process we use to bring experience into conversation with the wisdom of the Christian heritage. Unless we weave together material from the sources in a way that allows for give-and-take between our experience and the heritage, one that allows for surprises and insights in both directions, our reflection will be boring and pedantic.

Our habitual processes for interpreting life can interfere with correlating our experience and the wisdom of the Christian tradition in two ways. First, they can lead us to draw from the tradition source only data supporting positions we already hold. These may be positions about human existence or about the tradition itself. For example, if I hold the position that God primarily is a judge, I may be inclined to draw from the tradition stories and sayings presenting God as judge of human beings. For a dynamic correlation, however, we need to be willing to encounter data from the tradition source, and from the other sources, that challenge, revise, contradict, or deepen currently held positions. Such openness allows our correlation to create a real conversation between our experience and the rich resources of wisdom that Christianity offers us.

Our approach to the Christian heritage can create another obstacle to dynamic correlation of our experience with the tradition. When we approach the Christian heritage as a collection of timeless rules, abstracted from their original context and designed to be applied directly to our lives without consideration of differing historical contexts, we make correlation impossible. This orientation leads to a one-way monologue, from the tradition to our experience. It changes the Bible into a timeless manual applicable by any Christian to all situations everywhere. Using the Bible like a manual turns it into a magic talisman, like a rabbit's foot to bring luck or a cross worn around the neck to ward off enemies. Approaching the Scriptures this way transforms the Bible into an object that obstructs rather than communicates the Word of God to Christians.

The Bible is not a magic book. It is a collection of writings that tells the story of God's dealings with the Hebrew people and later with those Jews and Gentiles who accepted Jesus of Nazareth as the Messiah. It also tells how those people responded. When read and heard in a contemporary community of faith the Bible still conveys God's Word. It does so when the stories and people and situations it contains become alive to us and resonate with our stories and situations. Correlation is the way we create a context for this living conversation to occur.

In fact, the Bible itself is the fruit of theological reflection. The early Jewish and Christian communities uncovered the meaning of their experience, including for the earliest Christians their experience of Jesus of Nazareth, using the authoritative religious traditions, cultural concepts, and social structures of their day, their own positions, and their lived narratives. For example, the Acts of the Apostles, chapter 10, relates how the Apostle Peter changed his position on the question of whether or not the salvation God worked through Jesus was for the Jews alone or also for the Gentiles. Acts includes visions and revelations in its presentation of Peter's process of theological reflection, but these elements do not change the fact that Peter went through a process of reflection on this question, a process in which he correlated his lived experience (action source), tradition, and positions. In fact, theological reflection on the question of whether Jesus' salvation was for the Jews alone or for all creation preoccupied the Christian community for its first one hundred years and more.

The structure for correlation in a theological reflection design, then, is important. It creates the context for a dynamic conversation between our experience and the wisdom of our Christian heritage. In the correlation step of a theological reflection design, we want to bring the material from the source with which we begin the reflection into an energized conversation with the material from the other sources. This holds regardless of the source with which we begin the reflection.

Strategies for Correlation

Common Theme

The simplest way to correlate data from two or more sources is to use one or two questions to address the subject matter taken from each source. Comparing, contrasting, developing, and extending the responses to those questions provide the conversation. This approach works especially well if the design for reflection is built around a particular theme. For example, in a reflection around brokenness, two questions, slightly reframed for each source, can be used:

Action Source:
- What seemed hopeless in that situation where you were broken?
- Was there anything about your brokenness that now seems a gift?

Tradition Source:
- In this story, for example, woman with a hemorrhage (Mark 5:25–34), what seems hopeless in the woman's situation?
- What about the situation might be seen as a gift?

Culture Source:
- How is brokenness presented in popular films? (Talk about films people have seen.)
- Do these films present any possibilities of gift in the brokenness?

The reflection can continue by comparing, contrasting, developing, and extending the responses to these questions from all of the sources.

Here is a second example of a thematic organization for correlating with common questions, built around the theme of vocation or calling. First, material from the sources of action and tradition is identified and selected using questions related to the theme of vocation or calling. For example:

Action Source: Narrate a situation in your life when you felt called to do something.
- What was this like?
- How did you feel?
- How did you respond?

Tradition Source: Find two stories in Scripture of people being called. Read these stories.
- What was each one's situation like?
- Do the stories give indication of how each one felt?
- How did each respond?

Notice that the questions used to identify selections from each of the sources are similar. They pick out or identify both events of being called and also the thought and felt dimensions of those experiences.

The material from the two sources is correlated by developing the analysis and exploration of the data identified from each source. For example, the explicit correlation step in the reflective process might look like this: Compare the stories of call from your own experience and from the tradition.

- What are the similarities?
- What are the differences?
- What seems to be central to vocation or calling in this material?

This example gives a simple correlation between material from action and tradition. The correlation could be extended to include data from the culture and position sources. Whether or not we chose to do so would depend on the purpose of the reflection, the skill level of the group, and time available for reflection. For instance, the following questions would bring material on the theme of vocation or calling from the culture and position sources into our reflective process:

Culture Source:
- Does the culture of educated, affluent citizens of the First World include a concept of calling or vocation?
- What is it?
- How is it communicated?
- By what processes are people called to do things?
- What in this culture supports people to respond to calls?
- What in this culture may obscure calls?

Position Source:
- What have you believed a call from God would be like?
- What do you think it should be like? Why?

If the reflection is extended to include elements from culture and positions, the correlation becomes more extensive. The conversation would be fueled by data from all the sources and by identifying similarities, differences, key patterns, themes, or questions for further exploration in it.

In these examples of simple correlation, a single theme and set of questions create the commonality that makes a conversation among the sources possible. Materials from each source was identified around the respective themes of brokenness and vocation, though the theological code words were not used. The data from each source was explored and correlated using the thematic focus.

Correlation, then, provides a framework for allowing material from the different sources to be considered in terms of resonances, patterns, conflicts, and more. Notice that the conversation moves back and forth among the data that have been gathered from the sources.

Questions Behind Classic Doctrines

The example above uses the theme *vocation* to structure a correlation. That theme is drawn from the Christian heritage. All Christian themes, including those significant enough to be considered doctrines or fundamental teachings of the tradition, offer resources for building correlations.

Christian doctrines are answers to basic and, perhaps, universal human questions. But most Christians have learned doctrines as information, not as answers to classic human questions. When the doctrinal themes are separated from the context of their originating questions, they can become irrelevant and mute at best, and at worst, oppressive and threatening. Doctrines, divorced from their human context, too easily become ideological tools for dividing the world into those who are saved and those who are not.

An example from the United States of such ideological use of doctrine is the way the Baltimore Catechism dominated religious education for generations in the Roman Catholic Church. Children memorized answers to questions, often remembering them by question number, not question content. Somewhere along the way, however, teachers forgot that the catechism questions supposedly were connected to the children's experience. Or, if they did know it, they saw no need to point that fact out to the children. Generations of Roman Catholics received valuable information about doctrinal themes but were provided no guidance for correlating that information with their own lives.

The human questions behind classic doctrines or Christian themes offer another strategy for creating engaging correlations. We need to return to classic Christian themes and uncover once again the questions they address. We need to ask: What is this Christian theme about? To what human experience is it related? The classic Christian themes—creation, sin, grace, judgment, eschatology—represent the tradition's shorthand answers or accumulated wisdom in response to fundamental human questions.

Consider the theme of creation. This doctrine is concerned with fundamental views of and orientation to reality. It is concerned with basic premises about how the world is constituted. The Hebrew Bible's creation stories tell us that God pronounces creation to be good. Do we see it that way? In our daily living do we experience the world as fundamentally good? When we ask ourselves what life is like or what the structure of reality is for humans and the earth, how do we answer? How does our local or national culture answer? What answer do the actions of our lives suggest? The question behind the theme of creation is an important human question. In theological reflection it provides a common frame of reference for correlating material from the sources.[1] Let us look at some of the possibilities offered by other major Christian themes.

Sin is the doctrine concerned with the distortions and apparent or real wrongness in existence. What do we experience as destructive, tension-producing, tempting, and guilt-inducing in our lives? What seems needlessly and senselessly wrong in our world? What suffering do we see that is unreasonable and unnecessary?

Judgment, more easily understood today as crisis and conversion, is the doctrine concerned with the moments of recognizing one's participation in the distortions of existence. Judgment is about those moments when our view of reality and our way of being in the world are corrected. What has stopped us dead in our tracks and forced us to see ourselves as we really are in relation to ourselves, others, the earth, and the transcendent?

What evokes ruthlessly honest self-assessment in us, such that we find ourselves bidden to change and grow? How does our society respond to events such as war, riots, rape, and freezing deaths of homeless people that might call for national self-assessment?

Salvation is the theme concerned with those forces that set our individual and corporate lives on the path toward life again. Salvation involves those people, insights, and situations that help us to shift our course and move on to a new, more fitting, and richer way of being in the world. Those things that make life bearable in difficult times, which allow us to resist oppression and unjust suffering, which lead us to celebrate, which give us the inspiration and courage to be our best selves, all mediate salvation, in its root meaning—healing.

The doctrine of God deals with ultimacy. What is the ultimate power of the universe? What is its nature? Is it totally self-contained? Is it personal? Impersonal? Does it desire? Is it related to people and to the earth?

Eschatology is the theme focused on final fulfillment, what happens at the end of time. What is the best possible outcome? What do we hope for? What will be the fitting conclusion to all lives and all of history?

Ecclesiology is the theme concerned with human community at its best. The church, as the community of those who believe, love, and hope, in and because of Jesus, is called to model authentic human community for the world. What is the quality of relationships in authentic human communities? In what way do such communities embody what is truest about human beings and the human/divine relationship? How does our local Christian community respond to the call to be an authentic human community?

We have related some Christian themes to the human situations and questions that they address. This approach demonstrates that doctrinal themes are the Christian community's best wisdom or perspective on human experience formulated in a given time and place. Taking the time to think about the human context of Christian themes is an excellent way to develop a friendship with the Christian tradition. It further enhances our ability to create conversations between experience and the wisdom of our Christian heritage.

When we use the questions behind classic Christian themes to correlate data from sources, we gather the *perspectives* on that theme from each source. A perspective is an angle of vision on or perception of something. It refers to the way a questions, situation, or an issue looks and feels from a particular standpoint. Each source for theological reflection—tradition, positions, culture, action—contains characteristic ways of approaching and interpreting reality. Each one, then, constitutes a standpoint with differing perspectives on reality. When we use a question behind a classic Christian theme to structure correlation in a reflection, then, we get the perspectives on that theme from each source.

An illustration will help clarify. I may share an incident for reflection from my life that is captured in the image, "stuck in the mud." If I ask "What is the world like?" of the image, "stuck in the mud," the answers, for example, "constrained, limited, slippery," provide the perspectives on existence in the particular experience that I shared. If I brainstorm material from the tradition source evoked by the image, "stuck in the mud," for example, the disciples after Jesus' death and before he appeared to them, and then ask of some of that data, "What is the world like?," I begin to uncover perspectives on those kinds of experiences in the tradition. Similarly, if I then ask, "What does our culture say about being "stuck-in-the-mud?," for example, "You got yourself into this mess, now get yourself out of it," I begin to gather culture perspectives on "stuck in the mud" experiences. When I begin to compare, contrast, and elaborate the answers, I uncover perspectives on the meaning of existence from the different sources.

By using perspective questions that avoid religious code language, by asking, for example, "What is existence like when?" rather than "What is the doctrine of creation from which you acted in that situation?," we corral our habitual meaning-making processes, giving ourselves some space for surprise. If we use religious code language in the questions with which we explore data from a source, we may be tempted to give a "correct" answer, most likely a position we already hold or think we should hold.

Perspective questions, or questions developed from the human questions behind classic Christian themes, work particularly well in designs where reflection begins with group members sharing any incident or situation from their own lived experience that invites them to further reflection. When a group starts in an open-ended way the facilitator cannot build the reflection around a previously chosen theme. If the facilitator has an understanding of questions behind classic Christian themes, she can choose one or more of them as appropriate to plumb the experience that was shared. In such a situation using perspective questions allows the reflective process to develop organically. The task of the facilitator here is gently to guide the group through the reflective process, relying on the natural flow of the movement toward insight. Using perspective questions in this way establishes a fertile setting for considering and questioning the crux of the incident presented for reflection and the tradition.

The following summary of a theological reflection shows how questions for correlation built from the human questions behind classic Christian themes can be used. The process described here is built on the movement toward insight and begins with a presenter narrating any incident he chooses from his lived narrative.[2]

> A member of the group shared an incident from the past week. Walking home from an errand he encountered a girl who was blind. He greeted her and asked her where she wanted to go. She was looking for a mailbox. He guided her to the postbox, then guided her back across the street and they parted. As he watched her walk away he thought, "I can see, what a gift."
>
> With the group's assistance the presenter chose to hone in on the last part of the incident, the point where he thought, "I can see, what a gift." His feelings that captured the incident were: joy, awe, wonder, privileged, gifted. The image that they suggested to express the crux of the incident was "looking at a butterfly."
>
> At this point, having identified the heart of the matter in the cluster of feelings and an image, the reflection group began using perspective questions to explore the heart of the matter and to put it in conversation with the wisdom of the Christian tradition:

What is the world like when one is looking at a butterfly?

Answers: whole, beautiful, delicate, awesome, full of hope, wonder-full, featherweight, rich, transformed, nonviolent, a journeying place, playful, light and free, sensuous, welcoming

What is being human like when looking at a butterfly?

Answers: childlike innocence, spontaneous, contemplative, joyful, wondering, filled with awe, grateful, friendly, gentle, quiet, playful, connected (feeling one with things), restored, rejuvenated, energized, knows belonging-being-at-homeness

What is negative when one is looking at a butterfly?

Answers: responsibilities; violence—all violence in the world, someone trying to capture the butterfly, fragility, feeling of being trapped, ugliness, rushing, endings, moths mistaken for butterflies, injury to the butterfly, sap, spider's web

Notice that a simple experience has been explored for the perspectives in it on the themes of creation (What is the world like when one is looking at a butterfly?), theological anthropology (What is being human when looking at a butterfly?), and sin or evil (What is negative when one is looking at a butterfly?). In this reflection, then, theological perspective questions have shaped the exploration of material from a single source, action.

Continuing with the example will show how the perspective questions build the correlation between material drawn from the action and tradition sources.

Having captured the heart of the incident in the image "looking at a butterfly," and then having explored it using perspective questions, the group bridged to the tradition source. The group went back to the image and sat with it to let the image resonate and evoke material from the tradition. They brainstormed the following list of material from tradition: "Consider the lilies of the field"

- the Transfiguration story, "It is good for us to be here."
- Resurrection
- "God has chosen the weak things of this earth to confound the strong."

- "If you but knew the gift of God."
- "Let the little children come to me."
- Lazarus

The group chose the passages from Matthew's Gospel on lilies of the field and the Transfiguration on Mount Tabor. For each of the passages the group asked one of the perspective questions that it had asked of the image: "What does the passage say to the question: What is a real *human* being, what does it mean to be truly human?" The answers included:

- trusting in Providence
- "getting" that we are loved and cared for
- having a mentality or orientation of gift
- longing to be satiated, to see beauty and take it in
- believing human beings are made for beauty
- having heart-sight, a gift of Christ that makes it possible for us to be grateful
- realizing people need profound experiences in life

Notice that the group now has two sets of answers to the question: What does it mean to be human or what is a *human* being? The answers are perspectives on that question from two sources: action—captured in the image, looking at a butterfly—and tradition—lilies of the field and the Transfiguration. The perspective question provides the common venue for the conversation between material from the two sources. So this reflection developed the group's theological anthropology, to use the tradition's technical term for a view of a *human* being.

Perspective questions, then, help to correlate data from the sources in two ways. First, they let the classic human questions behind Christian themes be the common framework for exploring information from sources. Second, by getting back to these classic human questions and avoiding theological code language, perspective questions help us to corral our habitual meaning-making processes and strongly held positions so that we can encounter the data from the sources freshly.

We have presented two strategies for correlating information from different sources: common questions based on a theme and perspective questions. These two strategies can be adapted for most theological reflection designs.

Identifying New Truths and Meaning for Living or How Do We Bring Insights Back into Our Lives?

The central task at this stage in developing a design for theological reflection is to provide a way for participants to identify what they will take with them from the reflective process. This is a transition step in the process that moves the group out of the correlation's exploratory conversation into a mode of judging and clarifying. It is also the transition from the group's process back to the lives of the individuals who make up the group.

Finishing the reflection example from the previous section provides one illustration of how to do this:

> The group reflected on the perspectives on *human* being from the action and tradition sources. The conversation was lively and time ran out. The reflection ended with the group taking these questions with them for personal reflection:
>
> • What is one thing that looking at a butterfly, the lilies of the field, or Mount Tabor says to you about what it means for you truly to be a human being?
>
> • Are you willing to claim that statement as your own position?
>
> The next week the group began its session by sharing some of their further reflection during the week.

This example of a theological reflection ended with the members of the group taking away a question to ponder during their personal reflective time, understanding that they would return to share some of the results of that further consideration with the group. This approach acknowledges that a reflection does not end when the session ends. Indeed because theological reflection works on us at many levels shaping our faith, we can expect insights and understandings to continue to develop.

Bringing some of that further reflection back to share with one's group is a good way to embody it, to take it out of our minds and hearts and enflesh it in speech or writing or art.

Possibilities for identifying and claiming new truths and meanings from a reflection are varied. What approach we use depends again on the purpose of the reflection, the parameters of the reflection, and other factors. Consider the following:

Write down one truth from this reflection that you will claim as your own position.

Complete this sentence: "The next time I experience myself as, for example, looking at a butterfly, I want to remember . . . ."

Complete this sentence: "The next time I find myself in a situation where, for example, the fire alarm goes off in my brain, I will . . . ."

Write quietly in your journal for five minutes.

Break into pairs and share what has been most meaningful, supportive, and challenging to you in this reflection.

Draw or sculpt the central truth of this reflection.

Describe for the group the three key characteristics of the question with which you are leaving this reflection.

Take five minutes to shape in clay the wisdom you have gleaned from this reflective process.

Move into a prayer service in which group members express the meaning of the reflection for them as they leave it.

Break the group into pairs and have the partners identify any intention that is emerging for them from the reflection.

The important point for the facilitator to remember is that those doing theological reflection need to identify concretely something that they will take with them back to their daily lives. That something need not be profound or earthshaking. A question, phrase for prayer, an image, or a changed position will do.

Sometimes what a person takes from a reflection will be major and require significant changes. In that case, the facilitator, preferably with the group, should work to help that person develop an appropriate plan and arrange appropriate support so that he or she can act on the new insight. An example of this is presented in chapter 4, under the subheading, "Planning."

Borrowing or Creating Designs

Creating processes for theological reflection becomes easier with practice. Our skill increases if, after using a particular process, we spend time reviewing the reflection asking ourselves: What worked? What did not work? What question might have made the process flow more easily? Such regular reviews help us to develop methodological self-consciousness.

Becoming aware of available resources for theological reflection also increases our methodological repertoire. Many study programs involve at least implicit theological reflection. A significant literature exists on social analysis, a form of theological reflection that begins with the social structural aspect of the culture source. The Resources for Theological Reflection contains some of these resources. Add to it the resources you already use.

The fundamental thing to remember when facilitating theological reflection is that the process is a human process. The goal is being openly and compassionately attentive to the group with which one works and using a particular design to help crack open for that group their own instinctive desire and drive toward theological meaning. Remember, the facilitator of theological reflection is the midwife of the movement toward insight.

Summary

The framework for theological reflection provides a structure that can guide assessment of theological reflection processes and the creation of new designs for reflection. It helps a facilitator organize the range of strategies available for focusing on experience, identifying the heart of the matter of an experience, putting the heart of the matter into conversation with the wisdom of the Christian tradition, and identifying new truths and meanings for our lives. Which options a facilitator chooses in designing a theological reflection depends on her or his purpose and other constraints discussed under the "five P's" in chapter 5.

The design for reflection, however, is not the point of facilitating theological reflection. The design is a structure or vehicle for reflection. The design provides a pattern that highlights the natural movement toward insight and nudges it in a theological direction.

Above everything else, the facilitator of theological reflection wants to provide designs for individuals and groups that create a context for insight. Designs that enhance and do not obstruct the movement toward insight's natural progressions are most likely to serve that purpose.

7

Conclusion

Christians are called to theological reflection: the artful practice of bringing our lives into conversation with our Christian heritage in a way that nurtures insights for us and for the tradition. We are called to engage our lives and our Christian heritage from a standpoint of exploration, willing to trust that God is present in our experience and that our religious tradition has something to give us. Theological reflection offers challenge and support, frustration and delight, growth and celebration to Christian individuals and communities who persevere in the practice.

Theological reflection liberates as we carry our life experiences to the tradition. It increases and strengthens the connection between our lives and our Christian heritage, weaving the two more strongly into a single story of faithfulness. Through theological reflection we acknowledge our own longing for meaning. Through theological reflection we embody the courage to wait joyfully for the gift of meaning, a gift that cannot be claimed as personal accomplishment.

Theological reflection requires that we move out of the opposed standpoints of certitude and self-assurance in order to welcome the insight that genuine conversation between our lived experience and our religious heritage brings. It calls us to a gracious revision of strongly held, but ultimately detrimental, beliefs and convictions. It opens us to a deeper appreciation of belief and commitments that have aided our living and our faith. It leads us to an awareness of all the ways that we have been faithful to the gospel in our lives. In short, theological reflection calls us to a religious maturity that is life-giving for us and for our Christian heritage.

Whether or not theological reflection results in conviction, confirmation, or deepening appreciation of our own and others beliefs and actions, it always brings change. It disposes us to being transformed by God's power in God's time, and to being instruments of the kingdom. It impels us, individually and communally, to increased knowledge, greater consciousness, and critical perceptive sensibilities in relation to the self, family, community, and tradition.

Above all else theological reflection binds us to truth and meaning far deeper than any individual or generation can understand. It allows the tradition to transform us as we share good news with the world. If we are not so transformed, the tradition will die and we with it, mere caricatures, if not actual opponents of what Jesus called us to be when he spoke about the reign of God and the community of the kingdom (Matt. 13).

The world needs adult Christians who engage in theological reflection. In First World nations, Christian groups are heavily involved in political movements, often bitterly divided, and generally unable to explain their vision to anyone who does not share their presuppositions. On a global scale Christianity is shifting from being a primarily Western Hemisphere phenomenon to a worldwide and predominantly non-Western one. This shift is bringing changes in Christianity greater than those it went through when it moved from being a Jewish sect to a religion of the Gentiles.[1]

In this situation of massive transition in the Christian body, with all the conflict that great changes entail, Christians must become skillful at describing and reflecting on their experiences. The ability to reflect together on the meaning of our experiences in light of our faith in Jesus of Nazareth will allow us to identify the common values and vision behind particular beliefs and practices. Such reflection will make it possible for the Christian community to negotiate this transition intact with the vitality to continue to spread the good news of the gospel.

The call to theological reflection is not a call to an alien activity. Rather, it responds to the human drive to find rich and true meaning in our lives. Deliberate and self-conscious theological reflection builds on the ordinary way that we come to meaning, a process we have described as the movement toward insight. Our capacity to find meaning in our lives increases as we become aware of this process for making meaning.

The movement toward insight provides a foundation on which to build a basic framework for theological reflection. This framework offers a way to understand how theological meaning is made. It can help us find our way through religious texts, sermons, or tracts. It gives us resources for clarifying and further crafting our own theological vision in a way that is both critical and faithful to our Christian heritage.

This book has explained theological reflection using the movement toward insight and the framework for theological reflection in order to make this resource accessible to adult Christians. It includes processes of theological reflection in order to make such reflection available to adults who are willing to take their experience and their tradition seriously. That combination, taking both our experience and our tradition seriously, is the key to releasing and receiving the power of the Christian religious heritage that we claim.

Notes

Introduction
1. Leslie Silko, *Ceremony* (New York: Penguin Books, 1986), 126.
2. John Shea, *Stories of God* (Chicago: Thomas More Press, 1978), 41–49.

Chapter 1
1. David Tracy, *The Analogical Imagination* (New York: Crossroad, 1981), 99–101.
2. Tracy, 108–9.
3. Richard Feynman, *Why Do You Care What Other People Think?* (New York: W. W. Norton, 1988), 60–62.
4. John Shea, *The Spirit Master* (Chicago: Thomas More Press, 1987), 173–79.

Chapter 2
1. Shea, *Stories of God,* 15–16.
2. Charles Davis, *Body as Spirit; The Nature of Religious Feeling* (London: Hodder and Stoughton, 1976), 1–17.
3. John Dunne, *The House of Wisdom* (New York: Meyer Stone Books, 1988), 160.
4. Mary Gerhart and Allan Russell, *Metaphoric Process: The Creation of Scientific and Religious Understanding* (Fort Worth, Tex.: Texas Christian University Press, 1984), 94.

Chapter 3
1. Shea, *Stories of God,* 15–16.
2. Patricia O'Connell Killen and John de Beer, "'Everyday Theology': A Model for Religious and Theological Education." *Chicago Studies* (22 August 1983), 191–206.

3. This process is taught in the Education for Ministry Program described in the Resources for Theological Reflection.
4. Tracy, *Analogical Imagination*, 125.

Chapter 4
1. Tracy, *Analogical Imagination*, 125–26.
2. Ursula Le Guin, *Dancing at the Edge of the World: Thought on Words, Women, Places* (New York: Harper & Row, 1989), 3–6.

Chapter 5

Chapter 6
1. The Education for Ministry Program uses this approach.
2. This example comes from a reflection group of six people that met weekly for a year. The group used a reflection process known as the microscope method, which was first described and used in the Education for Ministry Program.

Chapter 7
1. Karl Rahner, "Toward a Fundamental Theological Interpretation of Vatican II," *Theological Studies* 40 (1979): 716–27.

Resources for Theological Reflection: An Annotated Bibliography

The resources included in this bibliography provide a map into the literature on theological reflection. This literature comes from a variety of fields, among them religious education, liberation, feminist, and fundamental theologies, spiritual direction, and ministerial education. Ministers and scholars in a broad range of fields understand the crucial significance of bringing human experience and the Christian heritage together in a dynamic conversation. No mature and vital faith can develop without the practice of theological reflection. This makes it a crucial activity for the individual Christian and for those ministers who walk with them on the journey of faith.

This bibliography includes three kinds of resources. Some directly address skills for leading theological reflection. Others provide theoretical frameworks for understanding theological reflection. Other items have been included that exemplify good theological reflection. The bibliography is not exhaustive. Many of its items contain additional bibliographic resources.

Programs

Center for Theological Reflection. P.O. Box 86035, Madeira Beach, FL 33738–6035. (813) 397–5477. The Center for Theological Reflection publishes materials to help ministers connect their experiences to their theology.

Education for Ministry. The Education for Ministry Program is a four-year small-group program of theological education by extension. It is the largest such program in the English-speaking world. Information about the program and facilitator training, which focuses primarily on leading theological reflection, is available from EFM, School of Theology Extension Center, University of the South, 735 University Avenue, Sewanee, TN 37383. (615) 598–1439.

EDUCARE. A network of religious educators developing and supporting alternative methods of education. They offer workshops on theological reflection and consultations for parishes and organizations incorporating theological reflection into their programs. EDUCARE, 2561 N. Clinton, River Grove, IL 60171. (708) 453–8298.

Institute of Pastorial Studies. The Institute offers workshops and some courses on theological reflection. The Institute of Pastoral Studies, Loyola University of Chicago, 6525 N. Sheridan Road, Chicago, IL 60626. (312) 508–2320.

Theory of Theological Reflection and Practical Guidance

Buttitta, Peter K. *The Still, Small Voice That Beckons: A Theological Reflection Method for Health Ministry.* Chicago: Peter Buttitta, 1992. Developed from Buttitta's experience working with parish nurses and in hospital chaplaincy, this practical presentation of theological reflection provides both theory and useful exercises. It was written particularly for people in the health-care professions who want to reflect on their work in light of Christian faith.

Fischer, Kathleen R. *The Inner Rainbow: The Imagination in Christian Life.* New York: Paulist Press, 1983. A most accessible introduction to the role of imagination in Christian faith. Fischer explains imagination and its role in connecting to Scripture, deepening prayer, and sorting out moral issues. Particularly useful for understanding imagination in theological reflection.

Green, Laurie. *Let's Do Theology: A Pastoral Cycle Resource Book.* London: Mowbray, 1990. Written from her experience in pastoral ministry in cities in England, Green presents a detailed introduction to doing communal theological reflection involving social analysis. Particularly helpful in presenting the theory of social analysis and practical guidelines on how to use it in communities.

Groome, Thomas H. *Christian Religious Education: Sharing Our Story and Vision.* San Francisco: Harper and Row, 1980. Written from a religious education perspective, Groome presents a "shared praxis" approach to theological reflection. Particularly helpful for settings where the leader is the primary carrier of knowledge about the Christian heritage.

Groome, Thomas H. *Sharing Faith: A Comprehensive Approach to Religious Education and Pastoral Ministry.* San Francisco: Harper and Row, 1991. Expands the "shared praxis" approach from religious education to other aspects of ministry.

Holland, Joe and Henriot, Peter. *Social Analysis: Linking Faith and Justice.* Maryknoll, N.Y.: Orbis Books, 1984. This best-known introduction to social analysis is clear, concise, and contains practical directions.

Holmes, Urban T. *To Speak of God: Theology for Beginners.* New York: Seabury Books, 1974. One of the earliest books to explain theological reflection for nonprofessional theologians. It contains an especially detailed explanation of sources for theological reflection.

Hug, James E., ed. *Tracing the Spirit: Communities, Social Action, and Theological Reflection*. New York: Paulist Press, 1983. This collection of essays explains theological reflection and describes how several groups actually have been doing it.

Keen, Sam. *To a Dancing God*. New York: Harper and Row, 1970. One of the earliest resources on telling our stories and using imagination, this classic is still a valuable resource for leaders of theological reflection.

Killen, Patricia O'Connell and John de Beer. "'Everyday Theology': A Model for Religious and Theological Education." *Chicago Studies* 22 (August 1983): 191–206. This essay presents the four-source model for theological reflection used in this book. It develops ways to think about the sets of sources for theological reflection in different settings. It gives a checklist of questions to think about in designing methods of theological reflection.

Killen, Patricia O'Connell. "The Practice of Theological Reflection in Small Faith Communities." *Chicago Studies* 31 (August 1992): 189–96. Concisely presents the essential elements necessary to create a context for theological reflection in which adults can come to insights.

Killen, Patricia O'Connell. "Assisting Adults to Think Theologically." *PACE* 22 (February 1993): 7–14. Gives a rationale for theological reflection and the elements required to create a context for theological reflection that can allow adults to have significant insights in terms of their own faith journeys.

Kinast, Robert L. *Caring for Society: A Theological Interpretation of Lay Ministry*. Chicago: Thomas More Press, 1985. Kinast exemplifies and then explains his method of theological reflection. His method incorporates insights from process theology more explicitly than those of other practitioners listed in this bibliography.

Kinast, Robert L. *Let the Ministry Teach: A Handbook for Theological Reflection*. Madeira Beach, Fla.: Center for Theological Reflection, 1992. Kinast's handbook gives practical how-to suggestions and examples for developing theological reflection. Those coming from a field education background will find his approach particularly amenable.

Manual for Mentors. Sewanee, Tenn.: School of Theology Extension Center, University of the South, 1993. The *Manual* is distributed to participants in theological reflection training offered by the Education for Ministy Program. The *Manual* contains several proven theological reflection processes.

O'Shea, John, Declan Lang, Vicky Cosstick, Damian Lundy. *Parish Project: A Resource Book for Parishes to Review Their Mission*. London: HarperCollins, 1992. This field-tested resource provides step-by-step instructions to lead a parish community through theological reflection about its mission. Its clear presentation of the pastoral cycle is especially useful for groups wanting to include theological reflection in their pastoral planning.

Shea, John. *An Experience Named Spirit*. Chicago: Thomas More Press, 1983. A theological reflection on the church and the presence of the spirit in the community of the church by a contemporary master of pastoral theological reflection. Shea presents his own method of theological reflection in the book. Read it both for its insights and to see how a master does theological reflection.

Shea, John. *The Spirit Master.* Chicago: Thomas More Press, 1987. A careful exploration of how faith is evoked and shared through interactions of fascination. Shea uses his own method of reflection in making his exploration. Read for what he says and for how he does his reflection.

Shea, John. *Stories of God: An Unauthorized Biography.* Chicago: Thomas More Press, 1978. One of the finest introductions to theological reflection, putting human experience and the Christian heritage together. Shea is particularly fine on narrative and human experience.

Shea, John. "Introduction: Experience and Symbol, An Approach to Theologizing." *Chicago Studies* 19 (Spring 1980): 5–20. An especially insightful piece on how symbols from our Christian heritage resonate with human experiences.

Whitehead, Evelyn Eaton and James D. Whitehead. *Method in Ministry.* New York: Harper and Row, 1985. This is a classic presentation of theological reflection for pastoral ministers. The Whiteheads present a tri-polar model of sources and a general process for accessing those sources and carrying out a theological reflection. The text also includes chapters that are examples of theological reflection done on several different topics.

Wingeier, Douglas E. *Working Out Your Own Beliefs: A Guide for Doing Your Own Theology.* Nashville: Abingdon Press, 1980. Written for lay persons, Wingeier's slim volume contains very practical exercises at the end of each chapter. The book explains theological reflection especially for Christians from the Protestant traditions.

More Theological Reflection Theory

Davis, Charles. *Body as Spirit: The Nature of Religious Feeling.* London: Hodder and Stoughton, 1976. Davis provides an excellent presentation of how human feeling is related to human knowing and insight. One of the early classics in the movement to retrieve the ordinary human experiences that ground good theology.

Dunne, John S. *The Reasons of the Heart: A Journey into Solitude and Back Again into the Human Circle.* Notre Dame, Ind.: University of Notre Dame Press, 1978. Dunne's work needs to be savored and experienced. He provides an expanded theoretical presentation of the movement toward insight as a method for theologians.

Dunne, John S. *A Search for God in Time and Memory.* New York: Macmillan, 1967. One of the earliest texts written on theological reflection beginning from our life stories. Well worth the effort.

Dunne, John S. *The Way of All the Earth: Experiments in Truth and Religion.* New York: Macmillan, 1972. Here Dunne uses his method of reflection to offer a way of engaging in dialogue with religious wisdom traditions different from one's own.

Farley, Wendy. *Tragic Vision and Divine Compassion: A Contemporary Theodicy.* Louisville, Ky: Westminster/John Knox, 1990. Written primarily as an exploration of how we can talk of the goodness of God in light of the horrors of the twentieth century, Farley's methodology illustrates good theological reflection. She shows particularly how to put biblical and cultural resources into conversation with one another.

Hellwig, Monika. *Whose Experience Counts in Theological Reflection?* Milwaukee, Wis.: Marquette University Press, 1982. A clear statement of the issues involved in using human experience as a source in theological reflection.

Killen, David P. and Patricia O'Connell Killen. "Theology in Its Natural Environment: Issues, Implication, and Directions." *New Blackfriars* 67 (June 1986): 277–87. Looks at the consequences for ministers and the church of taking theological reflection in local settings seriously.

Mueller, J. J., S.J. *What Are They Saying About Theological Method?* New York: Paulist Press, 1984. Introductory presentations on the methods of major twentieth-century theologians. Helpful for locating methods of pastoral theological reflection within the larger discussion of theological method.

Novak, Michael. *Ascent of the Mountain, Flight of the Dove: An Introduction to Religious Studies.* San Francisco: Harper and Row, 1971. This book still stands as one of the best explanations of human experience, its narrative structure, and the way stories are received and created by human beings as we live our lives.

Schreiter, Robert. *Constructing Local Theologies.* Maryknoll, N.Y.: Orbis Books, 1985. Excellent theoretical presentation on the relationship between theology and the social sciences. It is particularly useful for those who want to understand how human cultures are structured and the ways culture influences theology.

Tilley, Terrence W. *Story Theology.* Theology and Life Series 12. Wilmington, Del.: Michael Glazier, 1985. An insightful presentation of narrative and story as essential to our Christian heritage. Explains why theology has become interested in narrative. Helps readers to find the narrative structures in the biblical and theological traditions.

Tracy, David. *The Analogical Imagination: Christian Theology and the Culture of Pluralism.* New York: Crossroad, 1981. A detailed presentation of the theologian's multiple tasks in a pluralistic culture. The chapters on encountering classics are most useful for theological reflection.

Theological Reflection and Biblical Materials

Brueggemann, Walter. *The Bible Makes Sense.* Atlanta: John Knox, 1977. An understandable presentation of how to read the Bible for themes and questions. An excellent presentation of how to engage Scripture and not manipulate it.

Brueggemann, Walter. *Hope Within History*. Atlanta: John Knox, 1987. Superb essays exemplifying how to do theological reflection beginning with biblical resources.

Kinast, Robert L. *If Only You Recognized God's Gift: John's Gospel as an Illustration of Theological Reflection*. Grand Rapids, Mich.: William B. Eerdmans, 1993. Shows how a process of theological reflection is embedded in the gospel itself and invites us to encounter the text through that process.

Wink, Walter. *Transforming Bible Study: A Leader's Guide*. Nashville: Abingdon Press, 1980. Sound direction and practical guidance for using biblical material in theological reflection.

Literary and Autobiographical Resources for Theological Reflection

Autobiographical and literary works often deal with questions about the meaning and nature of life and the individual's purpose. They model good description and exploration of human experiences. Many exemplify good theological reflection.

Bender, Sue. *Plain and Simple: A Woman's Journey to the Amish*. San Francisco: Harper and Row, 1991. Explores questions of personal identity in an encounter with a strongly bonded religious community.

Buechner, Frederick. *The Sacred Journey*. San Francisco: Harper and Row, 1982. A model of moving from personal experiences to the theological heritage to uncover the richer meaning of that experience. Enjoy the engaging journey of faith but read more for how Buechner moves from his own experience to the Christian heritage and back again.

Buechner, Frederick. *Now and Then: A Memoir of Vocation*. San Francisco: Harper and Row, 1983. Continues the autobiographical theological reflection begun in *The Sacred Journey*.

Buechner, Frederick. *Telling Secrets*. San Francisco: Harper and Row, 1991. Continues the autobiographical theological reflections done in *Now and Then*.

Conway, Jill Ker. *The Road from Coorain*. New York: Vintage Books, 1989. Conway's autobiography provides an excellent example of how we reflect on our experiences and turn them into stories.

Dillard, Annie. *Holy the Firm*. New York: HarperCollins, 1988. Superb reflections on place, persons, and meaning. Dillard is a master at exploring the meaning of events in our lives. Read for her method of describing experiences and mining their meaning.

Dillard, Annie. *Pilgrim at Tinker's Creek*. New York: Bantam Books, 1974. An autobiographical presentation of a sustained period of reflection on ordinary experience.

Dillard, Annie. *Teaching a Stone to Talk*. New York: HarperCollins, 1988. This collection of essays exemplifies theological reflection on experience.

An Interrupted Life: The Diaries of Etty Hillesum 1941–1943. New York: Pocket Books, 1981. Though she died in the Nazi Holocaust, Hillesum's diaries live on as a presentation of a young adult's journey of faith against seemingly impossible odds. Fine examples of reflection on experience and valuable as well as a beginning place for one's own reflection.

Norris, Kathleen. *Dakota: A Spiritual Geography*. New York: Ticknor and Fields, 1993. Exquisite theological reflection on the geography and people of the western Dakotas. Insightful presentation of how religious traditions are shaped and shape communities and individuals. Norris models drawing on the sources of the Christian theological heritage to expand the deepen human experiences.

Silko, Leslie Marmon. *Ceremony*. New York: Penguin Books, 1986. The story of a young Native American man who undergoes a conversion and healing experience within his own culture's religious heritage. An extended reflection in fictional form on the place of tradition as life-giving and death-dealing in the late twentieth century.

Liberation Theology: Examples of Theological Reflection

Liberation theologians are committed to a method of reflection that takes account of the experiences of local communities of people. This form of theology is especially sensitive to social context and power relationships as part of the theological reflection process.

Aquino, Maria Pilar. *Our Cry for Life: Feminist Theology from Latin America*. Maryknoll, N.Y.: Orbis Books, 1993. Aquino's method and topic focus on the experience of Latin American women as it interacts with their religious heritages and cultural situations.

Freire, Paulo. *The Pedagogy of the Oppressed*. New York: Continuum, 1983. A classic presentation of reflection beginning with people's experiences, this work has influenced many methods of theological reflection.

Isasi-Díaz, Ada María and Yolanda Tarango. *Hispanic Women: Prophetic Voice in the Church*. Minneapolis: Fortress Press, 1992. Isasi-Díaz and Tarango elicit the stories of Hispanic women and connect them to theological themes. The book illustrates theological reflection.

Thistlethwaite, Susan Brooks and Mary Potter Engel, eds. *Constructing Christian Theologies from the Underside*. New York: Harper and Row, 1990. A collection of essays on doing theology from the experience and social-cultural settings of marginalized and poor people.

Feminist Theology: More Examples and Methods of Theological Reflection

Carr, Anne E. *Transforming Grace: Christian Tradition and Women's Experience*. New York: Harper and Row, 1988. An accessible and comprehensive introduction to the literature and issues of feminist theory and Christian theology.

Excellent for those who want to do theological reflection primarily with women.

Killen, Patricia O'Connell. "Rediscovering Women's Authentic Voices of Faith." *Sewanee Theological Review* 35 (1992): 365–79. Proposes that the process by which women come to voice and the process of faith development are connected. Suggests further that biblical resources offer an approach to the Christian heritage of suspicion and retrieval that is congruent with the dynamics of faith in Scripture.

Russell, Letty M., Kwok Pui-lan, Ada María Isasi-Díaz, Katie Geneva Canon. *Inheriting Our Mothers' Gardens: Feminist Theology in Third World Perspective.* Philadelphia: Westminster Press, 1988. Theological reflection on women's experiences with a focus on cultural contexts.

Sölle, Dorothee. *Thinking About God: An Introduction to Theology.* Philadelphia: Trinity Press Int., 1990. An introduction to central themes of the Christian tradition using a deliberate process of theological reflection beginning with experience. The text contrasts conservative, liberal, and liberationist perspectives on the themes. Read for Sölle's method.

Spirituality Resources for Theological Reflection

Coughlin, Kevin. *Finding God in Everyday Life.* New York: Paulist Press, 1981. A slim volume with valuable exercises that are easily incorporated into theological reflection processes.

Hanh, Thich Nhat. *The Miracle of Mindfulness!: A Manual on Meditation.* Boston: Beacon Press, 1976. An excellent resource for people who want to develop their ability to notice and describe their own experience in a nonjudgmental way.

Harris, Maria. *Dance of the Spirit: The Seven Steps of Women's Spirituality.* New York: Bantam Books, 1991. Offers a description of women's spiritual development as a process. Useful insights for working with groups of women who want to do theological reflection about their own experience. Also offers good resources for developing prayer services related to reflections.

Psychosocial Development and Theological Reflection

Belenky, Mary, Blythe McVicker Clenchy, Nancy Rule Goldberger, Jill Mattuce Tarule. *Women's Ways of Knowing: The Development of Self, Voice, and Mind.* New York: Basic Books, 1988. Written with reference to women, Belenky's and her colleagues' research provides insightful explanations of how both men and women relate to themselves, knowledge, and other people at various stages of development. Crucial reading for anyone who will be doing theological reflection with groups.

Whitehead, Evelyn Eaton and James D. Whitehead. *Christian Life Patterns: The Psychological Challenges and Religious Invitations of Adult Life.* New York: Crossroad, 1992. An excellent example of theological reflection using the authors' method and focusing on psychological themes.

Social and Cultural Accents in Theological Reflection

Baum, Gregory. *Religion and Alienation*. New York: Paulist Press, 1975. Particularly useful for understanding the way theologies are embedded in their social and cultural contexts and how that can lead to self-deception in theology and distortion of the Christian heritage.

Bevens, Stephen B. *Models of Contextual Theology*. Faith and Culture Series. Maryknoll, N.Y.: Orbis Books, 1992. An extensive analysis of how culture influences theology and of how different theologians use it as a resource for theology. Good explanation of the methods of a variety of theologians.

Clarke, Thomas, ed. *Above Every Name: The Lordship of Christ and Social Systems*. New York: Paulist Press, 1980. Essays of theological reflection on the gospel and the social structures of the United States. Useful for the variety of theological reflection methods used.

Coleman, John. *An American Strategic Theology*. New York: Paulist Press, 1982. Essays on theology for the United States context with particular attention to the intersection of the theological tradition and culture. Read for Coleman's insights and his method.

Whitehead, Evelyn Eaton and James D. Whitehead. *Community of Faith: Models and Strategies for Developing Christian Communities*. New York: Seabury Press, 1982. Crucial resources for thinking about the groups with which one does theological reflection. Also exemplifies an effective pastoral method of theological reflection on community issues.

Whitehead, James D. and Evelyn Eaton Whitehead. *The Emerging Laity: Returning Leadership to the Community of Faith*. Garden City, N.Y.: Doubleday, 1986. Exemplifies the authors' method of theological reflection while dealing with a serious topic, the nature of faithful leadership in the contemporary Christian community.